An Extraordinary God in Life

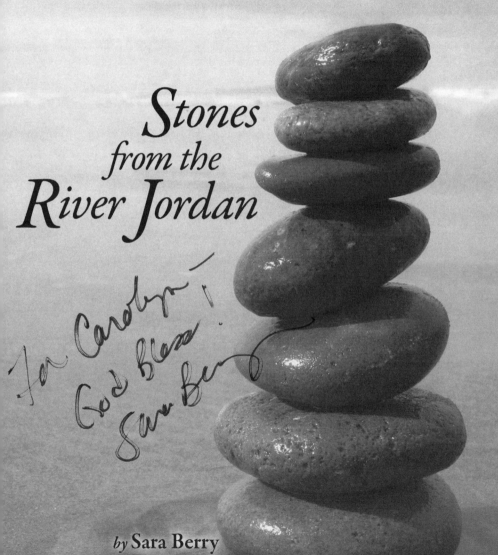

Stones
from the
River Jordan

For Carolyn~
God Bless!
Sara Berry

by Sara Berry

ISBN: 978-0-9816710-2-4

Printed in the United States of America

Cover Design and Interior Formatting:

Amy Lothorp and Lisa Sandroni, Tupelo, Mississippi

Cover Photo: Stephanie Rhea, Stephanie Rhea Photography, Tupelo, Mississippi, www.stephanierhea.com

Editorial Assistance: Yeazell Consulting, P.O. Box 383194, Duncanville, TX, 75138, info@yeazellconsulting.com.

Elaine Bunn, Tupelo, Mississippi

Bethel Road Publications, Tupelo, MS

www.bethelroadpublications.com

Dedication

Dedicated to my precious children:

Katie, Ellie, Joseph, Troy, and Joshua

As I share with you my Stones of Remembrance,
I can only imagine all the many Stones that our great Lord
will give to each of you over the coming years. I am in awe
of the way that I see each of you Reaching Up to God,
Reaching Out to others, and Remembering that Christ is
Lord. May He cement your feet to His path, all the days of
your lives. You are my great joy.

Acknowledgements

To Mont Berry

I can't imagine being on this road of life without you.
Thank you for your gift of faith, your perseverance, and
your godly example. Thanks for always supporting what
God calls me to do. I love you more than I can say.

"This is my beloved, and this is my friend..."
(Song of Solomon 5:16)

To Kelli Montague

Thanks for sharing so many of these experiences with me,
and for always being my faithful friend.
You are so beautiful to me.

To my parents, Kenneth and Nancy Ann Williams

Thank you for introducing me to Jesus, and for the godly
inheritance that you have passed down to me.

To Billy Still

Thank you for explaining and modeling what it means to
have Jesus as Lord, and for praying with me to receive a call
to ministry. You believed what God could do even when I
was an immature seventh grader.

To James and Caroline Loftin

Thank you for pointing out that the Great Commission was
for me. I praise God that we can still minister together.

What People Are Saying About Stones from the River Jordan

"Stones from The River Jordan is a must read! Sara Berry's weaving together of divine insight and practical application is a blessing that God uses to remind us of His provision in both the bountiful and scarce seasons of our lives. Sara reminds us that though the twelve stones were for the people of Israel crossing the Jordan with Joshua, the truths marked out by those stones were for God's people in every age. I wholeheartedly commend this book to you as an encouraging and uplifting read!"

Dr. Bryan D. Collier
Lead Pastor of The Orchard Church, Tupelo, Mississippi
Author of *Gentle Interventions, God's Graceful Work In Our Lives*

"As a career leadership educator, I have puzzled over the secrets to narrowing the maturity gap that is found everywhere in the lives of many of God's precious people. I have invested thousands of dollars, hundreds of hours of study, and years of exploration into the ways God makes us grow up into his likeness. Sara Berry, in the so many pages of "Stones," and with lasting wit and humility seems to charm the reader into adopting a grander view of their own circumstances, their own lives, their own God. Like one of her friends, perhaps an easily over-looked peasant, you may find yourself pulling back the coarse fabric of your life's back wall to find your own personally appointed mountain views that God wants you to reach up, reach out and remember."

Russell West
Professor at Asbury Seminary
Lexington, Kentucky

"Sit back and enjoy the honest reflections on life and Scripture of a Christ follower with global vision. I have known Sara for almost 30 years. She is a humble woman who walks her talk by listening carefully to the Spirit each day. She calls herself "ordinary." Watchman Nee would call her a "normal Christian." In the language of the Bible, she is faithful. Sara's witness is challenging and comforting, at times shocking but always believable. These chapters will help readers remember God's gracious acts in history, and become more involved in God's mission today."

James Loftin
President and Founder of FollowOne International
Orlando, Florida

"I have known Sara since she was 10 years old. Her friendship remains one of my life's most beautiful gifts. It doesn't surprise me to read of her: Reaching up as she invites young children to pray for a wounded butterfly while allowing the prayers of the same children to give wings to her healing. Reaching out as she peers through a wall in a Costa Rican slum accepting a young boys invitation to share the beauty of his life with her. Adding a stone of mourning to a pile of remembering while she prays 'Take my heart...'

'Reach Up, Reach Out and Remember' has helped me remember many things for which I am grateful."

Rev. Billy Still
Lead Pastor of St. Paul's United Methodist Church
Tuscon, Arizona

"Such an inspiring and encouraging book! Reading this book not only increases biblical knowledge, but enriches personal faith as well – as the author weaves profound truths from the Bible with her own life's experiences with the God she knows and loves so well."

Rev. Bill and Allen Bradford
Peru Mission
Trujillo, Peru

It's a meaningful event for me to discover a writer who can communicate profound truth simply and clearly. Sara Berry is my new discovery. To recommend a book that I don't have to mention who it is for...because it is for everyone...is a special joy. This is such a book. You will laugh, at least smile often as you read...maybe shed some tears. You will be challenged but also comforted. The Bible comes alive in a fresh way, and, if you are open, you will find direction and meaning for your life.

Maxie Dunnam,
former Chancellor and President of Asbury Seminary
Author of *The Workbook of Living Prayer*

Sara Berry leaves no stone unturned (pun intended!) in this book of studies on principles from the Word of God. Not only is she vulnerable in sharing her own weaknesses, but her deep, rich insights will be valuable to every reader. This wonderful book is sure to encourage your spirit, sure to provoke your thinking, sure to challenge your walk with Christ.

JJ Jasper,
National Radio Personality
American Family Radio

Reading Stones From the River Jordan is like a fresh wind of God's Spirit pouring encouragement and new faith into your soul. Sara Berry has a unique way of connecting God's Word with the practical, everyday challenges all of us face. Through her word, the Scriptures come alive in a new way. You'll finish the book and still keep replaying the beautiful stories and biblical insights in your mind. How refreshing to find an "ordinary person" that inspires us to do extraordinary things for God.

Christy Pierce,
Conference Speaker and along with her husband, Ben,
co-pastor of New Hope Peninsula Church, San Carlos, California.

Note from the Author

Dear Friends,

This book began when I read Joshua 3 and 4 in my daily devotion. From what I knew of Joshua, he had not always been this great, fearless leader. In fact, as I continued to study Joshua, son of Nun, I saw that he was a former slave...Even less than ordinary beginnings, yet called by God. And then the Lord began to lead me to other important Biblical characters, and there I saw a common thread...ordinary status. That is what they all had in common. And yet, God changed them and used them in extraordinary ways. He made the weak strong, the slave free, and the scared brave. And then it hit me: our ordinary ways, surrendered to his will, can produce extraordinary fruit. God loves to use the ordinary to produce the extraordinary. Because when extraordinary things happen in and through the ordinary, the glory goes to Him alone.

It is my prayer that you will be called to surrender to the Extraordinary God as you read this book. And that the surrendering will produce extraordinary results, despite your ordinary status. I have prayed for you this prayer:

> *"Now to Him who by the power at work within us is able to do far more abundantly than all that we ask or think, to Him be glory in the church and in Christ Jesus to all generations, for ever and ever. Amen"*

(Ephesians 3:20, RSV)

I am not a perfect person, nor do I have perfect understanding of our wonderful, mysterious God. My words are not perfect, but His Word is infallible. I hope that you find my words as a friend to friend conversation. I simply want to share my life and heart and my own Stones of Remembrance with my family and friends. If you are reading this book, I consider you a friend.

Most of all, I want to encourage you, my friend, to study God's Word daily which will, in turn, make you hungry for more. Psalm 34:8 says, *"Taste and see that the Lord is good."* I pray that as you taste of His Word each day, you will begin a life-long craving of it. This daily time in God's Word will lay a solid foundation for your life.

The bulk of this book can loosely fall under 3 different categories:
Reach Up
Reach Out
Remember

We must *Reach Up* to God first and foremost.

We then gain strength and purpose in *Reaching Out* to others.

But we must always *Remember* who He is and what He has done.

We must gather for ourselves Stones of Remembrance for we are a forgetful people. We are forgetful about who He is, what He can do, and what He requires. That is what this book is all about...it is about remembering. I want to remember who He is, what He has done and will do, and what He requires. I want to remember how extraordinary He is, and how, despite my ordinary status, He longs to do extraordinary things in me, through me, and for me....and in you, through you, and for you.

Peace and Joy,

Sara Berry
August 4, 2009

Table of Contents

Introduction
Who Am I?

The tears poured from my eyes as I drove down the highway, singing at the top of my lungs to the song blaring from my car radio:

Who am I, Jesus,
that You should call me by name?

That day, the sentiment of that chorus pierced my soul in an overwhelming way as I thought: *Who am I?* and as quickly answered my own question: *No one of significance; No one of power; No one of importance.*

I am a mom who drives a sticky SUV to and from the car lines of three different schools. Occasionally I am on time, but not very often. In fact, I sometimes forget appointments and every once in a while the lunch money. My kids are not perfect, although close to it in the eyes of their mom. I'm not very good at telling jokes, but I love to laugh at those who do. I have never been to seminary, although I have studied under others who are anointed and well-educated. And, I'm not tall or glamorous or even very graceful!

So before you begin reading this book, I need to tell you the truth about myself—I'm just ordinary.

My only "claim to fame" is that I am beloved of the Creator of the Universe, and have been called by Him. You are, too, whether you know it or not. I am a lover of God's Word and have diligently studied it, meditated on it, and tried to memorize it for 30 years. Most of all, I believe that I have been "taught of God," as the Scriptures promise to all His children who seek Him with all of their hearts. And I have been counseled by the Holy Spirit, which is also the inheritance of every believer. But, beyond those facts, I am 100% ordinary.

To prove my ordinary status, I will leave my pride at the door and tell you a story to illustrate my point. My husband, Mont, and I had been married for about six months when we moved to Nashville, Tennessee. After the move, I taught school for a year, then I started having babies…I had three children in less than three years. Later, I had two more, but the spacing was a bit more manageable! Mont was in residency at The Vanderbilt Medical Center and worked non-stop. We didn't have any family in town, and we were very broke. Needless to say, most days I felt like I was "in over my head."

One particularly trying day, Mont came home and I said, "I have got to get out of the house." So we put all the kids in their car seats and headed to my favorite store—Big Lots! Because we were broke, we couldn't buy anything, so we just pushed the kids around in the cart and walked the aisles, looking. We had been in the store for only a few minutes when Mont's beeper went off. He borrowed the Big Lot's phone, because that was before everyone had cell phones. He looked disturbed when he hung up the phone. The call was from the Vanderbilt Hospital operator saying that the police had called them because the alarm at our house was ringing.

Mont left the kids and me at Big Lots to go check out the source of the alarm. When he got to our house, the policeman was outside with his gun pulled, looking in the windows. He said, "Looks like you've had a robbery." Mont unlocked the front door and the policeman entered first with Mont following closely behind. The policeman said, "Yep. The place has been ransacked!" Mont looked around the front room and realized that it was just as we had left it before we went to the store. He quickly explained, "My wife has had a really bad day."

A Home for Him

Many times I have heard our hearts referred to as a home for Christ. We often experience times that feel like our spiritual house has been ransacked. Maybe is it because of a too-busy life, or a tragedy, or just apathy. Our response is usually to close the door to our hearts, and not deal with its mess. But God wants to lovingly and patiently help us to put our spiritual homes—our hearts—in order.

When I was fifteen years old, I had the great opportunity to travel to Germany on a summer student exchange program. The first day the group met together in preparation for the trip, I spotted this very cute boy. Smartly dressed in red and blue plaid pants and a red Izod shirt, I thought, "Who is that!?" In the good Lord's wonderful plan, I was assigned to sit beside this good-looking boy on the long plane ride to Germany.

That's right! Seated next to me in his lovely Late-1970s attire was Mont, my future husband. That trip to Germany was obviously pivotal in my future. And not just because I met my future spouse, but also because of the many lessons that I learned.

I was living with a German family, and thankfully the mother of the house could speak English, because I couldn't speak one word of German. On the last day of our visit, my American friend Cathy and I decided to venture out on our own, taking the public bus into the city in order to buy presents for our host families. Now, I grew up in a small town in Mississippi and had never even seen public transportation. But, because we had been on the bus a couple of times with the host family, we thought we could handle the journey alone. We made it into town without any complications, bought our presents, and then boarded bus #26 for the return trip home.

We had been traveling awhile before I realized that nothing looked familiar. I told Cathy that I was concerned, but she said it looked familiar to her so we kept talking and did not pay much attention to the ride. A short while later the bus came to a complete stop. We looked around and realized that we were the only two left on the bus and didn't recognize anything outside the bus. We went to talk to the bus driver, but he couldn't speak English so the conversation was pretty short! He kept saying, "Sprechen Sie Deutsch?" which means, "Do you speak German?" I tearfully replied, "I don't speak Dutch! Just take me to Langenstrauser Street!"

Finally, through hand motions, he told us that we had simply come to the end of the line, and after a short wait, we were on our way back. *You see, I was on the right bus, but I was going in the wrong direction.*

In thinking about a personal relationship with Jesus, I believe that we can ask ourselves two questions…

1. Am I on the right bus?
2. Am I going in the right direction?

Are you on the right bus?

First, are you on the right bus? I believe that our life in Christ is a wonderful, amazing journey which lasts our entire lives. However, you simply cannot experience the journey if you have not climbed aboard the "bus". The journey begins at salvation, and is fueled by making your personal relationship with God the highest priority. To experience all the wonderful things that God has for you, you must meet Him in a personal way by acknowledging sin and your need for a Savior.

Just as in any relationship, there will be highs and lows in your relationship with Christ. An important time in my spiritual walk came when I realized that just because that "good feeling" went away, didn't mean Jesus went away. In Joshua 1:5, God says, *"I will never leave you nor forsake you."* I have been a Christian for more than 30 years and I have always found that verse to be true.

It may seem strange to approach this topic of salvation to someone who willingly picked up this overtly Christian book, but sometimes we go through all the motions but never really "get it". That was my husband's story. Mont grew up in a wonderful family who also happened to experience many difficulties. Mont was the hero child. He was always a good guy. He did all the right things, and he always went to church. When he was a sophomore in college, he was a counselor at a Fellowship of Christian Athletes camp. A guy came to speak at the camp, and during his talk Mont realized that though he was the counselor, he had never really "gotten on the bus". He prayed that night and his life was forever changed.

Amazing Grace

Recently, my eight-year-old son, Troy, asked me to sing to him when I went to tuck him in bed. This was particularly special to me because when Troy was younger he had a very different opinion about my singing. I would often rock him for a while before putting him to bed. Each time I began to sing, he would place one chubby finger over his lips and say, "Shhhh!" As he grew older, he got more used to my "joyful noise" (maybe not beautiful, but at least joyful!). Once he even asked me why I had never become a professional singer. (If you could hear me sing, you would realize how funny this is!) I couldn't help but think that his ears must just be stuffed with love.

On this particular night he requested "Amazing Grace," so I lay down with him and began to sing. As I was singing I was thinking about these beautiful and familiar words. When I came to the second verse, I began to analyze the words. Truthfully, I had never really liked that verse because I didn't really get the first part:

'Twas Grace that taught my heart to fear
And Grace my fears relieved…

I thought, *how does Grace "teach my heart to fear," what's up with that?*
And then suddenly I realized that it is His love that shows us
our sin, and our weakness, and our need for a Savior. And it is
not to make us feel bad about ourselves but to shout the truth
that only through His grace can we be saved. This knowledge
relieves our helplessness and our hopelessness and our fears of
not being accepted.

I have written a program for children called Bug Club. BUG
stands for Being Under Grace. Each week of the program the
children review four basic truths about God's Grace…

- We don't deserve it
- We can't earn it
- Jesus bought it for us
- It's free

And I realized that the verse in the song is summarized in those
four points.
'Twas Grace that taught my heart to fear…

- We don't deserve it
- We can't earn it

By themselves, these two truths certainly teach our hearts to fear.

But then there's…

- Jesus bought it for us
- It's free!

And Grace my fears relieved…

These two truths relieve our fears, and make us realize that His grace truly is amazing!

Are you going in the right direction?

Secondly, we must ask ourselves, "Am I going in the right direction?" More of us may fall into this category than the first. I have many times. I became a Christian as a little girl when I knelt beside my bed and prayed with my daddy. I believe that God saved me at that point. However, when I was a teenager, I finally understood lordship and that Jesus wants to be both Savior and Lord of every aspect of our lives. Often, God has shown me different areas of my life that I have not surrendered to His lordship. He shows me through His Word, through prayer, and through other people. At that point, I confess through prayer that I am going the wrong way, turn around, and begin going in the right direction.

All this is relative to the story that we will be studying about the nation of Israel—the Israelites were on the right bus. They were God's people, but for 40 years they were going in the wrong direction. Let's back up just a little and remember some of the highlights of the story.

The Israelites were in slavery in Egypt for many generations, but were always looking for a deliverer to rescue them. And God chose Moses who was used to lead the people out of Egypt and deliver them from the bondage of slavery. They witnessed miraculous, powerful things in the midst of all this, including the fact that God parted the Red Sea and the people crossed on dry ground.

But here comes the sad part. Israel had to cross the Jordan River to enter the Promised Land. Many historians believe that it only took about two weeks to get to the Jordan River the first time. God had promised that He would lead them to their own special place, flowing with milk and honey. So, having witnessed mighty miracles only two weeks prior, they were set to enter the Promised Land.

Holy Numbers

Now let me stop for a moment and explain something that I think is really cool about reading the Scriptures. There are many references in the Bible to certain key numbers. I call them "holy numbers". Some of the most common are three, seven, 12, and 40. The number three can be classified as holy perfection like the Trinity—Father, Son, and Holy Spirit. The number seven indicates completion and perfection—like the seven days of creation. The number 12 often encompasses the family of God, representing all God's people, and reminds us of the covenant or unending promise of relationship between God and his people—like the 12 tribes of Israel or the 12 disciples. The number 40 is often a number of cleansing and preparation for the extraordinary—like the flood in the days of Noah which lasted 40 days and 40 nights, or when Jesus fasted 40 days in the wilderness before He began His ministry. Keep those numbers in mind as you read through this book.

When the Israelites got to the Jordan River the first time, they sent out 12 spies (Remember, 12 is a representation of all God's people and a sign of the covenant). They crossed the Jordan into the Promised Land to scout out the territory. They came back with samples of wonderful fruit, but also with a bad report.

Deuteronomy 1:22-32 tells us that all of the spies sent into the land agreed that the land was good. But ten of the spies began to tell of the difficulties that they imagined would be there. They saw evidence of a group of people that were so large that they considered them to be giants. They said, "We seem like grasshoppers in our own eyes" compared to them. Only Joshua and Caleb believed God and stood up for the Lord and for truth. This is what they said:

> "The land we passed through and explored is exceedingly good. If the Lord is pleased with us, he will lead us into that land, a land flowing with milk and honey, and will give it to us. Only do not rebel against the Lord. And do not be afraid of the people of the land, because we will swallow them up. Their protection is gone, but the Lord is with us. Do not be afraid of them." (Numbers 14:7-9)

Joshua and Caleb were courageous because of who God is, not because of who they were. What they saw in the Promised Land convinced them that God's promises were true and trustworthy.

Fear overcame all the rest of the people. In spite of the good evidence that the people saw, they chose to focus only on the obstacles. They set their minds on the potential difficulties and on their own strength, or lack thereof. As a result, they had to wander for 40 years (Remember, 40 usually indicates preparation and cleansing.) Because they did not trust God they could not receive all the wonderful things God had for them. In the end, only Joshua and Caleb would have the privilege of entering the Promised Land, because only Joshua and Caleb believed God.

Chapter 1
Reach Up, Reach Out, and Remember

When Jesus was asked which of all the commandments was the greatest, He replied:

> *"'...Love the Lord your God with all your heart and with all your soul and with all your mind.' This is the first and greatest commandment. And the second is like it: 'Love your neighbor as yourself.'"* (Matthew 22:37-39)

This passage summarizes three basic truths that the Lord speaks to us in His Word:

Reach Up

Reach Out

Remember

We must first and foremost Reach Up to God and love Him

with all of our heart, soul, and mind. Eternal, abundant life does not occur until we take that initial step of Reaching Up. And Reaching Up should continue throughout our lives.

Reaching Up equips us to obey the second greatest commandment, Reaching Out to others.

And the courage and the strength required to fulfill both of these two great commandments comes from Remembering who God is, what He has promised, and what He has instructed.

Joshua continually learned the value of these three simple truths. When we first hear of Joshua, we find out that he was a former slave of Egypt, an aide of Moses, and that he spent much of his time in the tent of meeting worshiping God. This time of worship was preparation for the great purpose that God had for him later in his life. He reached up to God.

Reach Up

Joshua is a person with whom I can relate. He outwardly appeared so strong and courageous, yet inwardly must have dealt with fear and insecurity, confusion and discouragement. Repeatedly, God told Joshua, *"Be strong and courageous, do not be terrified, and do not be discouraged, for the Lord your God is with you wherever you go"* (Josh. 1:9). In the first chapter of the Book of Joshua we see that God told Joshua three different times to "Be strong and courageous," and three different times God reminded Joshua that He would be with him, and that He would never leave him or forsake him. And that is just in the first chapter!

Why did God have to tell him to be strong and courageous so many times? I think it is because Joshua was an ordinary man called to an extraordinary job by his extraordinary God. And because he was ordinary, just like me and you, he waxed and waned between great seasons of faith, courage and confidence, and fear, doubt, and discouragement.

In the midst of it all, Joshua knew where to go for help. Courage is not the absence of fear, but the ability to press on despite the fear. And Joshua knew that true courage comes from the Source of all good things—God.

Reach Out

Joshua learned to overcome his fear through reaching up to God, which equipped him with the courage, strength, and confidence to reach out to others. In the Bible, we see many evidences of Joshua doing what he was called to do: he worshipped, he fought battles, and he was an aide to Moses. He did the work that God prepared for him. And sometimes the calling changed—he went from being a slave to being an aide to being a leader. We, too, need to first reach up to God, so that then we are equipped to reach out to others through whatever giftedness or circumstances God provides for us.

Ephesians 2:10 says, *"For we are God's workmanship, created in Christ Jesus to do good works, which God prepared in advance for us to do."* The Greek for the word, "workmanship," often has the connotation of a "work of art". This signifies that you are God's masterpiece! And that He has created you for a very extraordinary work!

Remember

As Joshua kept on faithfully reaching up to God, then reaching out to others, he was also asked to go one step further; he was called to Remember. We find out in Deuteronomy that throughout their years of wandering, the Israelites faced many obstacles. One battle, in particular, was a very difficult one to fight. During that battle, everyone had a particular role, and Joshua's role was to lead the fighting. After the battle was won, through a miraculous series of events, God told Moses the following:

> *"Then the Lord said to Moses, 'Write this on a scroll as something to be remembered and make sure that Joshua hears it, because I will completely blot out the memory of Amalek from under heaven.' Moses built an altar and called it The Lord is my Banner. He said, 'For hands were lifted up to the throne of the Lord. The Lord will be at war against the Amalekites from generation to generation."*
>
> (Exodus 17:14-15)

Why do you think that God wanted Moses to make sure Joshua heard all of the details of the victory? Because God knew what the future held for Joshua. He knew how He would use Joshua to finally lead the people into the Promised Land. He knew that Joshua would face these enemies again. He knew that this was an extraordinary job, and He knew that Joshua was ordinary. Joshua needed to remember in order to have the courage and strength to face the days ahead.

Roadblock on the Way to Promise

After many years all the fearful, unbelieving generation in Israel had died off, and just the children of that generation remained—all except Joshua and Caleb. In all that time the Bible tells us that God fed them with manna which faithfully fell every day. And neither their clothes nor their sandals ever wore out in all those years. And He never left them. After 40 years of wandering in the desert, their time of cleansing and preparation was over. Once again, Joshua found himself at the banks of the Jordan River. And once again, he sent spies out to scout out the territory.

When the spies returned, the news was good. They said to Joshua, *"The Lord has surely given the whole land into our hands; all the people are melting in fear because of us"* (Joshua 2:24). Joshua must have thought: *That's good news. Then why is my heart pounding so?* He must have told himself over and over: *Remember what Moses said. Remember what the Lord Himself told me: "…Be strong and courageous, for you must go with this people into the land that the Lord swore to their forefathers to give them, and you must divide it among them as their inheritance. The Lord Himself goes before you and will be with you; he will never leave you nor forsake you. Do not be afraid; do not be discouraged"* (Deut. 31:7, 8).

No wonder the Lord had to repeat the statement over and over. Be strong. Be courageous. Do not be terrified. Do not be discouraged. How can a former slave, now leader, overcome such fear? "Because I Am," says the Lord. "The Great I Am is with you. I Am promises to never leave you, nor forsake you. Don't forget Who I Am!"

Early in the morning, Joshua and all the people set out and traveled to the Jordan River. They camped by the river for three days. The significance of the number three is a subtle revelation of what was to come through these chosen people. Three days for them until they crossed into the long-awaited Promised Land, the land flowing with milk and honey.

Fast forward the story in time to their most precious descendant—three days in the tomb before the resurrection. Three days of death before the victory over death forever. After three days in the grave, the Savior conquered spiritual slavery and wandering and death forever for those who receive what has been won on their behalf. The ultimate Promised Land, ours for the asking. But like the Israelites, we must cross "the Jordan River" into faith receiving abundant life in the here and now. And, in the end, our final crossing will be more than we can imagine for all eternity.

For the Israelites, the Jordan River was a roadblock. It stopped the progression of the promise. After all the years of wandering, they were so close they could feel it! They could smell it! They were finally at the borders of the promise, but they weren't there yet. There was one more river to cross, but it was a doozey! At that time of year the Jordan River was at flood stage. Maybe a few of the strongest could forge the river—the spies made it across and back. But Joshua had the holy assignment of getting all of the people across the flood waters of the Jordan River, 40,000 men, not counting women, children and animals.

Stepping Out and Standing Firm
Joshua 3:5-7 tells us that:

> "Joshua told the people, 'Consecrate yourselves, for tomorrow the Lord will do amazing things among you.' Joshua

said to the priests, 'Take up the ark of the covenant and pass
on ahead of the people.' So they took it up and went ahead
of them. And the Lord said to Joshua, 'today I will begin to
exalt you in the eyes of all Israel, so they may know that I am
with you as I was with Moses.'"

Joshua was new to this leadership thing. Also, Moses had recently died, and maybe the people did not fully trust Joshua yet. I wonder if it was hard for Joshua to believe that the Lord would do something extraordinary in his life, despite his past. But God said it was coming!

After three days, the time had come. Joshua called for preparation. He told the people "Consecrate yourselves, for tomorrow the Lord will do amazing things among you" (Josh. 3:5). I imagine him saying:

"Get ready, people! I know you can't see it; I know that
you don't remember right now all the other mighty things
that He has done for us. I know that to some of you these
are just stories told to you by your fathers and grandfathers.
I know that none of you were there when the Lord sent the
plagues, or when we were delivered from the slavery of
Egypt, or when we crossed the Red Sea. But I was there. I
remember. Caleb remembers, too. Ask him. I know you
have never known life without manna, but I'm here to tell you
that is not the norm! I remember the days when we toiled
and labored for what little food we had. I remember the first
time I tasted manna. I remember. And that is why I know
that He is up to something! And when He says get ready,

dy! He is the great I Am; He is the covenant
of the promise. And He has promised that He
...into this Promised Land. I believe Him, because
...remember."

The people got ready. They consecrated their outward selves, while at the same time prepared and consecrated their inward selves. They cleansed themselves completely. They prepared heart and soul and body. And then they waited. And nothing happened at first until the priests got wet.

"Tell the priests who carry the Ark of the Covenant: 'When you reach the edge of the Jordan's waters, go and stand in the river.'" (Joshua 3:8)

The priests had to take that giant step of faith into the flooded waters of the Jordan River. We, too, sometimes have to take that step of faith before we see the results. Hebrews 11:1 says, *"Faith is the substance of things hoped for, and the evidence of things not seen"* (NKJ). What were the priests thinking when they felt the water soaking their sandals? When the clothing that had lasted for 40 years, but had not worn out, began to be heavy with moisture? But then it happened. They all heard the sounds of that great body of water peeling back. The water piled up in a heap a great distance away, at a town 20 miles upstream. And the priests kept walking, carrying the Ark of the Lord with them. They kept walking to receive all the great promises that they had waited so long to receive, for He who promises is faithful—always.

"The priests who carried the ark of the covenant of
the LORD stood firm on dry ground in the middle of the Jordan,
while all Israel passed by until the whole nation
had completed the crossing on dry ground." (Joshua 3:17)

The priests went first because they were carrying the Ark of the Covenant. This was a beautiful gold box that contained the presence of God. Of course, God is omnipresent, and we can't keep Him in a box, but there was a reigned-in holiness surrounding that box, because it was a concentrated portion of God's presence. Since Jesus completed His work on the cross, we don't need an ark. Now, God dwells in the hearts of men. We, too, can stand firm, no matter the trial or difficulty, if we remain in the presence of God.

As the priests stood firm in the middle of the Jordan, strengthened with the presence of God, the people followed. Were they afraid that the water would fall back on them? Did they run across in fear or walk quickly across in amazement? Regardless of their emotions at the time, they did just what the priests had done. They took that step of faith and kept going. When the priests carrying the Ark of the Covenant of the Lord got to the middle of the Jordan, they stood there until the whole nation had completed the crossing on dry ground. Scripture says, *"They stood firm on dry ground in the middle of the Jordan"* (Josh. 3:17). They stood firm in what had become their personal experience, not just the experience of their forefathers.

My mother used to always say, "God doesn't have grandchildren, just children." We can't rely on our parents' faith. We learn from them, but eventually we have to make it our personal experience. The priests could stand firm because the Ark of the Lord was holding the presence of the Lord Himself. So it was the Lord who held the waters back while the people crossed on dry land. The middle of the Jordan was surely the most dangerous spot to be. But, the Lord Himself remained in the place of danger, on their behalf, until all were safely on the other side.

This is one of many examples that show that He is our refuge, our shelter from every storm and our safety. He alone can do extraordinary things on the behalf of ordinary people. Just as the priests held the presence of God, so we as sons of God carry the presence of God in our very hearts and souls. Therefore, we, too, can stand firm in every dangerous and difficult place. We, too, can *"Be still, and know that [He] is God"* (Psalm 46:10).

Stones of Remembrance

When the whole nation had finished crossing the Jordan River, the Lord had another significant assignment. He told Joshua to select 12 men, one from each tribe, and instruct them to go back to the middle of the Jordan River and take up twelve stones from the spot where the priests stood firm. They were to then carry the stones over to the people. So Joshua obeyed. He called one man from each of the 12 different tribes, symbolizing that God's promises were for all the people, and that the generational covenant still was intact. The priests took the twelve stones from the Jordan and brought them up out of the middle of the river.

"That day the LORD exalted Joshua in the sight of all Israel; and

they revered him all the days of his life, just as they had revered Moses.
Then the LORD said to Joshua, 'Command the priests carrying
the ark of the Testimony to come up out of the Jordan.' So Joshua
commanded the priests, 'Come up out of the Jordan.' And the
priests came up out of the river carrying the ark of the covenant of the
LORD. No sooner had they set their feet on the dry ground than the
waters of the Jordan returned to their place and ran at flood stage as
before." (Joshua 4:14-18)

The stones from the river served a purpose as stones of
remembrance. At the Lord's command, Joshua said to the
people...

"In the future when your descendants ask their fathers, 'What do these
stones mean? Tell them, 'Israel crossed the Jordan on dry ground.' For
the Lord your God dried up the Jordan before you until you had crossed
over. The Lord your God did to the Jordan just what he had done to the
Red Sea when he dried it up before us until we had crossed over."
(Joshua 4:21-23)

The Lord wanted them to take the stones from the Jordan
because He knew they were a forgetful people. They were
forgetful about who He was, what He could do and what He
required. And, I am forgetful, too. That is what this book is all
about...it is about remembering.

And as we remember who He is and what He has done and
what He will do, He will begin to do extraordinary things. Why?
So that all will know that God is powerful and wonderful and
kind and merciful and loving. When they see us, and what God

does despite our ordinary-ness, God alone will be glorified.

"He did this so that all the peoples of the earth might know that the hand of the Lord is powerful and so that you might always fear the Lord your God." (Joshua 4:24)

Look at verse six again: *"In the future, when your children ask you, 'What do these stones mean?' tell them..."* As a mother of five, I know they will ask. I remember when our first daughter, Katie, was in the "sleeping bag phase". She really wanted to sleep with us, but was not allowed due to the principal of preserving the marital relationship and, if truth be told, due to a double-sized bed that only comfortably slept two. So the closest that she could finagle was sleeping in the hallway outside our room in her sleeping bag. This sleeping bag phase lasted for a year-and-a-half; which was fine with both mother and child, because her room was always neat, and I didn't have to wash the sheets!

So our nightly bedtime routine took place in the hallway. One night, as I was tucking her in (as much as is possible with a sleeping bag), she asked me to tell her a "missionary story". She loved to hear the true tales of our experiences on the mission field. So I obliged and told her the story of a jungle boy who loved Jesus. Towards the end of the story, she interrupted me with an odd question: "Mama, how does he get in there?" Racking my brain about the story, I came up short with what she was asking...how does the boy get in the jungle? How does he get in his hut? So I asked her what she meant. She replied, "How does Jesus get in your heart?"

I replied that you ask Him to enter your heart, you tell Him you are sorry for all of the things that you do wrong, and you ask Him to make you into a new creation. She quickly replied, "But…how does He get in there?" I thought for a moment, and then replied with a question to her. I said, "Katie, when you are outside playing on a windy day, do you see the wind?" "No, ma'am," she replied. Then I said, "But can you feel the wind on your face? Can you see the wind blowing the trees?" "Yes, ma'am," she replied. "That is what it is like to have Jesus in your heart; you can't see Him enter, but once He does, you feel His presence, and you see that He is working in your life."

We continued on with our nighttime routine: singing, hugs, water, etc. Just as I was about to leave the hallway, Katie quietly, but firmly, said, "I want to do that, Mama. I want to ask Jesus into my heart." So I returned to kneel beside her sleeping bag, and led her in a prayer to commit her life to Jesus. As soon as she prayed, she joyfully exclaimed, "I get it, Mama! It's like the song…" And she began to sing a heartfelt rendition of the beautiful song….

> I have decided to follow Jesus.
> I have decided to follow Jesus.
> I have decided to follow Jesus,
> No turning back, no turning back.
>
> Though none go with me, still I will follow.
> Though none go with me, still I will follow.
> Though none go with me, still I will follow.
> No turning back, no turning back….

As I left the hallway, I was overcome with the privilege that I had just experienced. I was there when she was born into this earth, and I was there when she was born again. In fact, that is why I began writing this book—for my children—because I didn't want to forget my own stones of remembrance.

Will you join me as I remember? I want to remember Who He is, what He has done and will do, and what He requires. I want to remember how extraordinary He is, and how, despite my ordinary status, He longs to do extraordinary things in me, through me, and for me—and in you, through you, and for you. Join me as I remember…

*Stones
of
Longing
Surrender
& Waiting*

Chapter 2
Longing

Longing is a feeling with which we can all relate. For all
of us there has been a season of life that was filled with that
desperate, empty feeling in the pit of our stomachs. We went on
about life, but there were very few moments that we found rest
from the longing. Let's look at a woman who dealt with feelings
of desperate longing year after year. Her name was Hannah.

We can label our longings with different names, but the
feelings are usually the same. The name of Hannah's longing
was "children". The source of her longing stemmed from an
ugly word that was far-reaching in its repercussions: barrenness.
Today, we refer to it as infertility. Many of you may relate to
that source of longing. Honestly, I have not. But I have walked
beside friends who have, and have partnered in their burden.

As I studied the story of Hannah, I realized that it matters
not what the source of longing is, the source of fulfillment is
always the same—life in Christ. So, as we study the story of one
particular woman's longing, I want you to fill in your own blank.

My longing is _____. What is it? What has it been? It matters not how you fill in the blank, because the lessons we can learn from Hannah's story will still apply. Let's look at it together...

"There was a certain man from Ramathaim, a Zuphite from the hill country of Ephraim, whose name was Elkanah son of Jeroham, the son of Elihu, the son of Tohu, the son of Zuph, an Ephraimite. He had two wives; one was called Hannah and the other Peninnah. Peninnah had children, but Hannah had none.

Year after year this man went up from his town to worship and sacrifice to the LORD Almighty at Shiloh, where Hophni and Phinehas, the two sons of Eli, were priests of the LORD. Whenever the day came for Elkanah to sacrifice, he would give portions of the meat to his wife Peninnah and to all her sons and daughters. But to Hannah he gave a double portion because he loved her, and the LORD had closed her womb."

(I Samuel 1:1-5)

Year after year Hannah's husband went to worship and sacrifice to God—this was not just a short-term problem. This was something that haunted her, and it affected her relationship with God. Each year the routine of worship and sacrifice was a huge part of their lives. It was their chance to be close to God. This was before Jesus died, and sacrifices were still necessary for a relationship with God.

When the day of sacrifice came, Elkanah gathered his family and gave a portion to sacrifice to each of his wives and children. Peninnah had children, so there were several portions on her side of the family score card. Elkanah loved Hannah, and felt sorry for her, so he gave her a double portion. But she still had less to offer to her God. In her mind, she was unacceptable to God, and because the system based the allotment of sacrifices according to the number of children one had, she probably felt that she could never measure up.

"And because the LORD had closed her womb, her rival kept provoking her in order to irritate her. This went on year after year. Whenever Hannah went up to the house of the LORD, her rival provoked her till she wept and would not eat. Elkanah her husband would say to her, 'Hannah, why are you weeping? Why don't you eat? Why are you downhearted? Don't I mean more to you than ten sons?'"

(1Samuel 1:6-8)

Hannah could not accept her lot in life or heal from her pain because there was a constant source of irritation rubbing salt in her wound. And she could not escape it. The source of irritation came from her household, and many tears were shed.

Let me stop right now and tell you about tears. In the Book of Revelation we learn that one day God Himself will wipe away every tear from our eyes. Psalm 56:8 tells us that He saves our tears in a bottle. Our tears are precious to the Lord. He sees and feels every one of them. And He has already done something about them. In Isaiah, as well as 1Peter, we learn that we are healed by His wounds. He wants to heal whatever hurts you have.

Year after Year

Like Hannah's situation, the source of our longing or difficulties often stem from our own households. Year after year we long for change in someone or something in our lives. Year after year it seems as if God is silent. My husband's brother, Lee Hunter, was one of the kindest young men you could ever meet. He was loving and easy to talk to. But he always seemed drawn to trouble and constantly wanted to push the limits. In college, he pushed further than he could handle and ended up with a severe drug addiction. Year after year we all prayed. Year after year we attended family sessions for yet another rehab center. Year after year he made promises that he was unable to keep. We all longed for change, for the miracle of deliverance.

The process of deliverance was disguised in tragedy. Lee Hunter had a terrible automobile accident which nearly killed him and left him crippled and forever changed. He had had diabetes since he was a child, and his unhealthy lifestyle over the years had contributed to complications in that area. While in rehab for physical therapy after his wreck, my father-in-law had the opportunity to share once again the truth of God's amazing grace. Lee Hunter accepted Christ that day, and in the months following described his new life in the following way: "I feel like there is a river flowing inside of me." What a beautiful description of what it feels like to be filled with the Spirit of the living God.

Three months later, Lee Hunter died from complications of

diabetes. His funeral was a celebration that God had won! Year after year we had prayed. Year after year we had longed for change. And God had heard every prayer and seen every tear. And He answered. Lee Hunter is finally free!

Our Deepest Needs

In I Samuel 1:8, we see that Hannah's husband, Elkanah, said to her, *"…Hannah, why are you weeping? Why don't you eat? Why are you downhearted? Don't I mean more to you than ten sons?"* Elkanah sounds like a sweet man, and we are told that he did love Hannah very much, but he just didn't get it. This had nothing to do with him. This was about a longing that Elkanah couldn't fill. Not just because he wasn't a child, but because this was about her and God. Hannah felt abandoned by God, that this longing kept her away from God. And it broke her heart.

Our deepest needs can only be met by God. No one and nothing can fill us in our deepest parts. And it is really disappointing when we try to place other people or things in that place of deepest need, because it never really meets the need. These substitutes might give us a temporary relief, but then we are back to where we started. Only a close relationship with Jesus can fill us up and meet our deepest needs.

> *"Once when they had finished eating and drinking in Shiloh, Hannah stood up. Now Eli the priest was sitting on a chair by the doorpost of the LORD's temple. In bitterness of soul Hannah wept much and prayed to the LORD. And she made a vow, saying, 'O LORD Almighty, if you will only look*

upon your servant's misery and remember me, and not for

get your servant but give her a son, then I will give him to the LORD

for all the days of his life, and no razor will ever be used on

his head.'"

(I Samuel 1:9-11)

Hannah began to make promises to the Lord. In bitterness of soul Hannah wept much and prayed to the Lord. And she made a vow saying, *"O Lord Almighty, if you will only look upon your servant's misery and remember me, and not forget your servant..."* (I Sam. 1:11). Hannah's main problem was that she felt like God had forgotten her. I have felt that way before—have you? Feeling forgotten until the Holy Spirit whispers truth once again to my heart.

God tells us in Isaiah that even if others forget us; He will not forget (Isa. 49:15). Although Hannah was afraid that the Lord had forgotten her, she promised that if He gave her a son, she would turn around and give him right back. She was vowing that she would devote her son to be a Nazarite.

A Nazarite was a person who was especially devoted and consecrated and set apart for God's purposes. A person could become a Nazarite in two ways: first, if the individual made a vow to become a Nazarite for a specified amount of time; and secondly, as a lifelong devotion following a vow made on their behalf by a parent before their birth.

A Nazarite would typically be recognized not only by their apparent devotion to God, but also physically, as they did not cut their hair, come into contact with the dead, nor partake of any alcoholic products. This type of vow made by the parent typically followed a revelation from God which announced the birth of the child. When Hannah spoke this vow, she was speaking in faith. It had not been announced to her that she would now have a child. This was her mustard-seed faith in action.

Being Misunderstood

"As she kept on praying to the LORD, Eli observed her mouth. Hannah was praying in her heart, and her lips were moving but her voice was not heard. Eli thought she was drunk and said to her, 'How long will you keep on getting drunk? Get rid of your wine.'

"'Not so, my lord,' Hannah replied, 'I am a woman who is deeply troubled. I have not been drinking wine or beer; I was pouring out my soul to the LORD. Do not take your servant for a wicked woman; I have been praying here out of my great anguish and grief...'" (1Samuel 1:12-16)

Even in her ultimate moment of surrender, Hannah was misunderstood by others. Eli saw her in her despair, and he assumed the worst—that she was in the temple, drunk with wine, because her emotion was so raw. He misunderstood in the very area in which she had made a vow to God. She had vowed to give everything to Him, and yet was accused of being a sinful woman. But what really matters is that God understood, and in time evidence was revealed of her pure heart and her faithful vow. God has defended her for thousands of years now as the evidence that His answer is there for all of us to see in His Word. He will come to our defense!

"Eli answered, "Go in peace, and may the God of Israel grant you what you have asked of him." (1Samuel 1:17)

Eli was there to see Hannah's surrender, because he was part of the ultimate plan. He would need to remember the scene in order to be a faithful player in the next phase of God's plan. And Eli was used of God to send Hannah a powerful, prophetic word. The word that God had for Hannah that day was "Go in Peace". Totally opposite of what she had been feeling year after year. Peace that passes understanding. And that is really what we all long for, isn't it? We eventually come to a point that we long for peace more than anything else.

Don't Worry

"Don't worry about anything; instead, pray about everything. Tell God what you need, and thank him for all he has done. Then you will experience God's peace, which exceeds any thing we can understand. His peace will guard your hearts and minds as you live in Christ Jesus."
(Philippians 4:6-7; NLT)

Don't worry about anything. Whatever it is that you filled in the blank a few minutes ago, please realize that even in that, God does not want you to be anxious.

But instead, pray about everything. Nothing is too small to talk to God about. You would laugh about some of the things that I pray about. Remember, if you think it, He knows it. So why not go ahead and talk to Him about it?

Then you will experience God's peace, which exceeds any-thing we can understand. That is what we really need. Peace in the midst of an impossible situation. Peace despite the reality. That does not mean we live in denial or avoidance of the problem. It means that we look to Him, because nothing and no one else can help us. The world offers only momentary distraction. God offers perfect peace. *"You will keep in perfect peace all who trust in you, all whose thoughts are fixed on you!"* (Isa. 26:3; NLT)

Eli said, *"Go in peace"* (I Sam. 1:17). There is action in the word "go". It's as if God wanted Eli to give Hannah the permission to live. Sometimes our problems and longings are so heavy that they weigh us down and we can't move forward. I have seen people even feel guilty about living joyfully in the midst of their problem. We can live in the midst of our longing or heartache by remembering Who God is. *"For He himself is our Peace"* (Eph. 2:14; NKJ). Peace is not found in a change of circumstances, or even in an answer to prayer. Peace is found in a person, God Himself.

Wendy's Story

Like Hannah, we all have experienced the difficult emotion of longing for something. Reaching Up to God will transform and purify our longings and bring comfort and strength in the midst of our longing. My dear friend, Wendy Collier, had her own difficult struggle, and I have asked her to share her story:

Bryan and I had been married for almost two years when we decided it would be a good time to "begin our family". With great excitement we began to pick out names and look at baby clothing and baby furniture—I even enjoyed looking at maternity clothes. I wanted to be pregnant. Bryan and I were the first of our siblings to marry so we thought it would be fitting to be the first to be expecting a baby.

Well, months went by and I slowly began to suspect a problem. That slow realization continued to unfold over the next seven years. 1 Samuel verse 10 says that, "In bitterness of soul Hannah wept much and prayed to the Lord". My soul became bitter bit by bit through those seven years. Both of my sisters-in-law became pregnant, my college roommate was expecting and yet we were being left out. Jealousy began to overtake my life. You see—I knew that the Lord was the giver of life and yet He was choosing to NOT give life to Bryan and me. Baby showers, infant baptisms and Mother's Day became unbearable and I began to hold every woman of child-bearing age at arm's length.

Hannah describes her feeling as "deeply troubled with great anguish and grief"—for me that was putting it mildly. A darkness came over my life like never before. Now that I look back I realize how much the Lord wanted to walk with me and comfort me and be my everything, but I wouldn't allow it. I was desperate and shameful and alone—unlike the rest of the fertile world.

I was totally consumed with fertility treatments and my pain. I prayed continuously for the Lord to take away the desire to have a child if that was not His plan for my life. I rationalized that my request was a noble one since God had commanded us to be fruitful and multiply. There was nowhere to go, no place to hide, and nothing to fill my time with that would alleviate the pain, despair and depression.

The years of infertility were a long and slow grieving process. I was grieving a loss—the loss of a dream—the dream of experiencing pregnancy, the dream of a biological child, the dream of seeing a child grow up, the dream of grandchildren, the dream of how life should be.

While Bryan was still in seminary—with no job—we drained our small retirement account and decided to go for broke and try in-vitro fertilization. In the weeks leading up to our in-vitro attempt we asked all of Bryan's classmates and families to pray for us and we had prayer service in our tiny seminary apartment asking God to give us a child. It was May 13, 1998—my 29th birthday—we received the results from our in-vitro attempt—negative. I had begged God to allow me to be a mother before I turned 30 and it seemed that time was running out.

Now, that all has sounded so desperate—and that I was—but the Lord didn't leave me there. Little did I know the plans He had for me. Up until that point it was pretty much all about me. I wanted to be pregnant. I wanted to be a mother. But, very quietly and slowly my heart began to change. I decided that I wanted to be a parent more than I wanted to be pregnant and the Lord had bigger plans than what I could ever imagine and the plans included many more people than just me.

Being an adopted child myself, my mother always said that God knew exactly which child she needed and which mother and daddy I needed. I didn't believe her until I was on the other end of the deal. Looking back I see that the events I want to share with you are not just happen-stance. These details were carefully orchestrated by my heavenly Father.

When Bryan and I came back to Mississippi in 1998 the Lord provided me with a part-time job at Gardner-Simmons Home for Girls working with a college sorority-sister of mine. My sorority sister gave me the name of an adoption agency in Indiana. In October of 1998 we made the trip up to Indiana to meet with the pastor's wife who started and managed the agency. We submitted a portfolio to be presented to birthmothers. In February of 1999 we received a call that there was a birthmother interested in us. It was not customary for the agency to let the adoptive parents know about the possibility until every thing was final because so many adoptions fall through.

A birthmother's decision for adoption isn't the easy way out. It is the most difficult decision they will probably ever face in life. It is a decision made out of love. Well, our birthmother wanted to meet us. This had never happened before with this agency. Of course, Bryan and I were very willing. I was willing to donate a kidney or cut off my right arm if need be. Thankfully, that was not necessary, and in April of 1999 (one month before I turned 30 years old) a beautiful baby girl was born. Our birthmother called to ask what we would like to name her. We named her Olivia Kate Collier. All those years Bryan and I wondered what our child would look like together. It has been the icing on our cake to have a daughter that looks just like her daddy with the coloring of her mother.

Fast forward two years. I received a call from our adoption agency asking if we were interested in adopting another baby—she needed to know in the next four hours—since the birthmother was due the next week. We had not applied to adopt again. We felt so blessed to be the parents of one; we had not considered being the parents of two. I told our social worker that it sounded good to me, but I needed to check with Bryan first. He immediately came home from the office and we prayed for the next four hours. We decided not to close any doors.

In August of 2001 our son was born. Again, the Lord amazingly orchestrated so many details to allow us to become Houston's parents. Houston's birthmother had lived a hard life, but during her pregnancy she accepted Jesus as her Savior and let Him be Lord of her life. Her pastor helped her move from Wisconsin to Indiana during her pregnancy to go to college and get a job. She was working with an attorney on a private adoption and already had an adoptive family picked out, yet she didn't have peace about it. She said that she knew the Lord had big plans for this child and she was not the one to help this little boy become who God wanted him to be.

During the last month of her pregnancy she found our adoption agency in the Yellow Pages and came into the office to meet with the social worker. There she saw a picture of Olivia that we had sent. She said, "That is what I looked like when I was a little girl. Tell me about that family." The social worker said, "Well, that family has not applied to adopt again." To which she replied, "Will you call and ask them?" How amazing! The Lord has entrusted to our care two precious children. Just like in Hannah's story we know that these children are not ours to own. They are the Lord's. We only have a short time to parent and influence them to be all God has for them to be. So, each night before prayers we have them repeat after us: "God has big plans for me". After seven years of heartache we have such joy. The Lord answered our prayers in very different ways than we had planned and in His timing. How perfect are His ways. How perfect is His timing.

Chapter 3
Surrender

Right after Mont and I married, we anxiously awaited the news of the residential match for Mont's specialty, Otolaryngology. The fact that it is a competitive field, and the fact that the news would determine where we would spend the next five or six years of our lives made the waiting very miserable.

We were leaving the country for a three-month mission trip, and we had arranged to find out the news about a week before it was announced nationally. We were in the Miami airport, about to leave the country, and we used the pay phone in the airport to call the National Otolaryngology Match Office. Of course, I had determined what the best plan would be and had already told the Lord what was best. You see, it made perfect sense to me for us to match in Jackson, Mississippi where we were already living, where we had close friends, and where the residency program was a whole year less than the Vanderbilt program. When Mont had done a month-long rotation at Vanderbilt, I never saw him. He hardly even had time to call me, and when he did, it was late at night after he had worked about 16 or 17 hours straight. We wanted to start a family in the coming years and I was sure that if Mont matched at Vanderbilt I would basically be a single parent. I was certain that God would see it my way.

I'll never forget standing beside Mont as he said to the lady on the phone, "Yes. Yes. That's right. Really? O.K. Thank you so much." He hung up the phone, and with eyes really big, turned to me and said, "I matched at Vanderbilt". My world came crashing down. I had only been a wife for one month, and any attempts at being a good wife collapsed with the news. I could not believe it! God did not do what I thought He would. He had not listened to me. He had ignored my input, my desires, and my "wisdom". I burst into tears and could not quit crying for the next three hours. Even after the tears stopped, I couldn't even talk about it for the next three weeks. I had no thoughts of this being the best situation for Mont, or that it would turn out the best for me and our future family. I was only sad and mad that it had not turned out the way I thought that it would and should.

Five months later, we arrived in Nashville and began to unpack in our new little house. I was nervous, but resigned to my situation. I had decided to quit fighting with God and buck up and endure the next six years. How wrong I was! The six years we spent in Nashville were some of the most wonderful years of my life. My first three children were born there. Mont's schedule was bad, but not unbearable. He learned to be a quality husband and dad despite the lack of quantity time. The habit of making every moment count endures today. We sowed seeds of friendship that are reaping a fruitful harvest even today, 15 years later. The friends we met in Nashville are still some of our very best friends, and always will be.

Maggie's Cross

One couple, Rivers and Ali Rutherford, have been particularly close to us. Though now Rivers has made quite a name for himself in the country music industry as a songwriter, at the time we were all struggling along together. Despite the financial difficulties, both Ali and I wanted to stay home with our young children. We came up with many schemes to make an extra dollar or two, all the while taking care of our little ones. Our children became fast friends as well and are still like siblings to this day. When we moved back to Mississippi after Mont's residency was complete, we committed to keeping in touch, which we have. Not long after we moved, I got a call from Ali. They were on their way to the hospital with their oldest daughter, five-year-old Maggie, who was very sick. The diagnosis was not good—meningitis. Maggie quickly fell into a coma and we didn't know whether she would live or die.

Mont finished seeing patients that day and then we left for Nashville to be with Rivers and Ali. I felt sick with worry over Maggie, as well as pain for what Ali, as a mother, had to endure. We arrived at Vanderbilt Medical Center expecting a scenario of despair and fear. I was completely surprised at what we found. I still remember Ali's face. It was radiant. She is naturally a beautiful person, but despite the tension and lack of sleep, her face was glowing. And it was glowing because she was experiencing something that I never expected to see—peace. I have never seen a more physical manifestation of a spiritual condition. Ali had completely surrendered her heart to the Lord, trusting that no matter what happened He was still on the throne. She trusted in His love for Maggie, and for herself. I was inspired by what I saw.

Weeks passed before Maggie was "out of the woods". In the end, she made a full recovery and is now a beautiful teenager who is deeply committed to the Lord Jesus.

Five years later, we were planning another trip to Nashville. This one would be marked with fun and joy. We were going to visit the Rutherford family for the weekend. Mont worked in his clinic the day before we left. He saw a patient that day which he did not recognize. When Mont entered the examination room, the patient said, "I bet you don't remember me". Being a very personable man, Mont hated to admit that he did not remember this patient, but had to reply truthfully, "I'm sorry, sir, but I don't". The man told him that he had seen Mont only once before as a patient five years prior. The man said, "I remember it, because you were about to leave to go to Nashville to see your friend's sick daughter. You asked me to pray for her. I did pray for her. Could you tell me…did she live?" Mont replied, "Yes! She did live, and in fact we are going to visit them tomorrow!" The man then reached in his bag and pulled out a beautiful hand-made cross. He said, "I'm so glad she lived! I made this for her. I brought it just in case. Could you give it to her?" We did, indeed, give Maggie that beautiful cross. We told her to use it as a reminder that God is a wonderful, sovereign God and He has great plans for her life.

In the Course of Time

As we continue our study of Hannah and her longing, we come to an amazing part of the story: When Eli spoke God's word to Hannah, she immediately changed. *"Then she went her way and ate something, and her face was no longer downcast"* (1Sam. 1:18).

Hannah's circumstances and problem had not changed, but she had changed in her soul. That is what happens when we surrender completely to God. Our surrender ushers in the Prince of Peace. Sometimes the Prince of Peace calms our storms. Sometimes He calms us in the midst of the storm. He calmed Hannah before he calmed her storm. And it was a miracle.

Hannah worshiped and went about her life, no longer desperate. *"Early the next morning, they arose and worshiped before the Lord, and then went back to their home...and the Lord remembered Hannah"* (1Sam. 1:19). We see no evidence here that her worship was hindered. And, *"...in the course of time Hannah conceived and gave birth to a son"* (1Sam. 1:20).

There is a lot of meaning in the phrase, "in the course of time". We don't know how long she still had to wait, but her waiting was different now. She waited in peace. Her surrender to God was real, and her life reflected the change. . "In the course of time"...not immediately, still time and probably more pain to go before the fruition of the plan, but her surrender and vow set the plan in motion. If she had had her answer earlier, she would not have been to the point that she could totally surrender herself and her son to the Lord, and all of history would have been different. God had an enormous, extraordinary plan for Hannah and the world through Hannah that was much larger than she could have imagined. And it really was worth waiting for.

Hannah gave birth to a son and named him Samuel, which means "the Lord hears". That is really what Hannah needed to know; that God heard her heart's cry. He did hear, and He does hear ours. One of the first questions that comes to our minds, but sometimes we are afraid to ask is, "Why did God let the longing go on for so long?"

You should not be afraid of expressing your questions and feelings to God. God created the emotions inside of you and can handle anything that you feel. You do not have to hide your feelings from Him, for He knows them already. The quicker we acknowledge to Him how we really feel, or acknowledge the questions that we have, the quicker He can transform our hearts with the renewing of our minds. Take everything to the Lord in prayer. When you pray, God always answers you. *"Before they call I will answer; while they are still speaking I will hear"* (Isa. 65:24).

God ALWAYS answers.

Sometimes He answers "yes."

Sometimes He answers "no."

Sometimes He answers "wait."

God sometimes answers no. Sometimes the no is because the thing we are praying for is something that is not right or good for us. God sometimes answers no because we live in a fallen world that will not be made right until the end of time.

God sometimes answers wait. God sometimes answers wait because the details for the fulfillment of our prayer are not in place yet. God sometimes answers wait because the glory He will receive will be even greater when the answer comes.
If God answers no or wait, we can rest assured that His ways are higher than what we can see right now. *"And we know that all things work together for good to them that love God, to them who are the called according to his purpose"* (Rom. 8:28).

My Children

Because of fear, I have had a hard time surrendering my children to the Lord. It took me a few years to really believe that God loved them more than I did. I remember my point of surrender concerning my kids. I was at Pickwick Lake when I felt overcome with a case of the "What Ifs". The more I thought about the future, the more fearful I became. I remember praying a desperate cry for help: "Lord, I need a word from you that I can hang on to." Though I don't really recommend this method, I simply opened my Bible and the first verse I saw was:

"As the rain and the snow come down from heaven, and do not return to it without watering the earth and making it bud and flourish, so that it yields seed for the sower and bread for the eater, so is my word that goes out from my mouth: It will not return to me empty, but will accomplish what I desire and achieve the purpose for which I sent it."
(Isaiah 55:10-11)

I prayed, "Yes, that is true. God's word will not return void. And I do pray God's Word over each of my children. But Lord, I need a word from you that is specific to them. Give me a word for my children." I flipped a couple of pages and my eyes fell upon the following verse: *"I will contend with those who contend with you, and your children I will save"* (Isa. 49:25b). I immediately felt an overwhelming peace flood my soul. The fear fled. The calm returned. I prayed, "Ok, Lord. I believe you. Help me with my unbelief." And whenever Satan tries to bind me again with fear concerning my children, I let my powerful God "contend" with the enemy, and I simply remember and believe.

A few months after this word from the Lord came to me; my family attended a revival at the First Presbyterian Church in Corinth, Mississippi. The speaker offered a time to come to the altar for those who wanted to receive Christ as Savior and Lord. All of a sudden my son, Joseph, jumped up and grabbed my hand and began pulling me down the aisle, all the while encouraging his cousin, Rebekah, to go, too. As I made my way down the aisle with my son to pray, very clearly to my mind came the precious words from the Lord: "I will contend with those who contend with you, and your children I will save."

A couple of years later, we had a little bit of a scare with Joseph. I had to take him to get a cat scan of his brain, because he was experiencing a lot of dizziness. I remember fighting off the "what-ifs" and praying instead, "Lord, I gave him to you a long time ago. I will not take him back now." That was a difficult prayer to pray. You see, it is very hard to surrender something to the Lord and not pick it back up again.

Elkanah and his family continued in their yearly ritual, but this year was different. Hannah stayed back. I always wonder if she was ever tempted to back out on her part of the deal she made with the Lord. But Hannah did what God had equipped her to do and then she gave Samuel back to God. Here she was at a time of surrender once again, yet this time she was different. This time she was confident in who she was, and Whose she was. This time she remembered who God was and what He was capable of. He had already done extraordinary things in her and through her, and now she was going to trust Him to do it again.

> "…they brought the boy to Eli, and she said to him, 'As surely as you live, my lord, I am the woman who stood here beside you praying to the LORD. I prayed for this child, and the LORD has granted me what I asked of him. So now I give him to the LORD. For his whole life he will be given over to the LORD.'" (1Samuel 1:25-28)

I imagine Hannah, gathering her courage, silently whispering a prayer for strength, and taking her young boy's hand, her precious answer to prayer, and saying, "Remember me, Eli? I was the one who was in such despair. Well, here is my answer to all those prayers. And I am giving him back to God, and to you. For his whole life, I won't take him back."

Chapter 4
Waiting

I remember a particular season of longing in my life. I was young and single, at times content and focused, and other times I was longing for more. My heart's desire was to be a wife and mother, yet God had not brought "the one" into my life yet. I wanted to give the Lord every part of my life, even my longings and desires. Yet that is often much easier said than done. I felt my heart moving toward one particular person, a young man that was one of my best friends. In fact, I met him on that plane heading to Germany. I had even told him one time that I wished he was a girl so that he could be one of my bridesmaids whenever I got married! The transformation of love in my heart from that of a best friend to much more was a very difficult transition. It did not help that he was a busy medical student who wanted to stay focused on his studies, yet gave just enough hints and encouragement to keep me hanging on hoping for more in the relationship.

My brother, Ken, had shared with me about the freedom of relinquishing our desires to the Father. He told me that he pictured his desires as a small box, like a gift. And in his prayers, he would offer the box, symbolizing his wants and desires, to the Lord. He would imagine leaving the box at the altar, and praying, "Not my will, but Yours, O God". So, through prayer, I brought my desires to God's altar time and time again. Yet I kept picking them back up, analyzing and trying to control them once again. And then one day, I read about burnt offerings.

It was February 14th, Valentine's Day, and once again I was tempted with discontent and sadness. I had begun reading the *One Year Bible*® as a new year's resolution and was tempted to skip the Old Testament reading because it seemed so irrelevant to me. However, I wanted to hold true to my resolution, so I trudged through the assigned reading. The reading that day was about the preparation of the altar. I began to pray, saying, "Lord, I've tried that. I have tried again and again to lay down my desires and my unfulfilled dreams and hopes and wishes. I have tried to lay down my sadness and heartache, but I keep picking it back up."

And then I read further about the preparation of burnt offerings. You see there were different types of offerings that the people presented to the Lord in the Old Testament. There were offerings of grain and first fruits, there were offerings of sweet smelling incense and drink offerings, and there were burnt offerings. And I began to think about the burnt offerings. If I offered my desires as a burnt offering, one of two things could happen. Either it would be something made beautiful, as silver refined in the fire, or it would be a black charred mess that

I would not want to pick back up anyway. So I prayed that my desires would be as a burnt offering.

I finally found that place of surrender. And the things that God had been trying to teach me during that difficult season suddenly began to form as truth in my heart. He was enough! He was what my heart longed for more than anything else. And, as time would tell, the burnt offering turned out to be a thing of beauty, refined by the fire of pain and surrender.

In Isaiah 61, we read prophesy about the Messiah, the one who would make all things new:

> *"The Spirit of the Sovereign LORD is on me,*
> *because the LORD has anointed me*
> *to preach good news to the poor.*
> *He has sent me to bind up the brokenhearted,*
> *to proclaim freedom for the captives*
> *and release from darkness for the prisoners,*
> *to proclaim the year of the LORD's favor*
> *and the day of vengeance of our God,*
> *to comfort all who mourn,*
> *and provide for those who grieve in Zion—*
> *to bestow on them a crown of beauty*
> *instead of ashes,*
> *the oil of gladness*
> *instead of mourning,*
> *and a garment of praise*
> *instead of a spirit of despair.*
> *They will be called oaks of righteousness,*
> *a planting of the LORD*

for the display of his splendor." (Isaiah 61:1-3)

In Jesus' first public sermon, He stood up and read this passage and said, *"Today, this scripture is fulfilled in your hearing"* (Luke 4:21). Many did not understand then. Many do not understand now. But if you have ever had those times of surrender and felt His refining fire burning off the dross in your life, you know that only Jesus can bring beauty out of ashes.

Within a month, the Lord had turned my situation totally around. He rather dramatically told this young man, Mont Berry, that yes indeed I was the one that He had prepared to be his wife. And yet, the refining fire had sealed my heart for my first love to be Jesus. And I have found throughout our years of marriage that keeping Jesus as my first love allows me to love Mont and my children more purely, more completely, and more abundantly than I ever could have by giving them first place in my heart.

In July of that year, I knew that Mont and I were going to be married, I just didn't know when. I was to meet him in Nashville where he was doing a rotation at Vanderbilt. The Thursday night before I left, I could not sleep because words kept rolling over and over in my mind. I got up and within five minutes wrote down what the Holy Spirit was stirring within me. It was basically a summary, in the form of a poem, of the great lessons I had learned through that season of my life. I wrote it down in calligraphy on nice parchment paper, rolled it up and put it in my backpack. I thought I would share it with Mont, if God so led.

That Saturday, we went for a long drive, as Mont expressed his need to "get out of town". Of course, I did not care where we were as long as we were together. We drove to Black Mountain, North Carolina and climbed the mountain trails to the top with its beautiful view. Mont told me that it was the place that he had prayed to receive Christ as his Lord and Savior. I reached into the bag, unrolled the poem and handed it to him to read. He read:

Though You Are Enough

Jesus, my love, my truest friend,
Joys you give me and pain you mend.
How can I thank you? How can I express
What's in my heart of gratefulness?

Though You are enough to satisfy,
You've given me another, in whom my trust can lie.
You've given me another love and friend
Who will stay beside me to the very end.

Though You are enough, my wholeness, I know,
You've given me someone faithful, someone I can hold.
Someone who my joys will share,
Someone who will see my pain and care.
Someone who loves You as much as I.
Someone who for Your Cause would die.

Though You are enough, I know it's true,
I thank You for this other love, so fresh and new.
And when the newness fades away

By struggles and pain that will come our way,
    We will still have You, our truest friend,
    To rekindle our love and make us one again.

Though You are enough, this truth will ring;
    Though I love You more, my Lord, my King;
    Though You are enough, that's plain to see,
Thank You, precious Jesus, for this other love for me.

After reading the poem, Mont reached into his backpack and pulled out a beautiful engagement ring, and asked me to marry him! Through the years, I have made a conscious effort to remember those lessons learned through that hard time. And I can truthfully say that Jesus is enough. I love Him more, yet He fills my heart with such an abundance of love for my husband and children, the depth of which I cannot even attempt to describe. Even through the difficult seasons of our lives our Lord is at work. He takes care to prepare us for our future. The waiting is often long and hard. But it is during those waiting periods that we experience the warmth of faith and the intimacy of friendship with the King of Kings. And His plans are always worth the wait.

Chapter 5
Longing Fulfilled

When Hannah delivered her precious young son to live in the temple with Eli, she was not filled with the sorrow that we would expect. Instead, she prayed a victorious, joyful prayer:

"Then Hannah prayed and said:
My heart rejoices in the LORD;
in the LORD my horn is lifted high.
My mouth boasts over my enemies,
for I delight in your deliverance.
"There is no one holy like the LORD;
there is no one besides you;
there is no Rock like our God.
"Do not keep talking so proudly
or let your mouth speak such arrogance,
for the LORD is a God who knows,
and by him deeds are weighed.

"The bows of the warriors are broken,
but those who stumbled are armed with strength.
Those who were full hire themselves out for food,
but those who were hungry hunger no more.
She who was barren has borne seven children,
but she who has had many sons pines away."'

(1 Samuel 2:1-5)

In the midst of this her second surrender, Hannah's heart was filled with praise and thankfulness. *"...those who were hungry hunger no more"* (I Sam. 2:5). The longing had been fulfilled! And the hunger made the feast all the better.

When I was a missionary in Costa Rica, my friend Kelli and I decided to fast and pray the first day of each month that we were there. This was a fairly big commitment because food had become quite a daily problem for me. I didn't like beans. It is very hard at mealtime in Central America if you don't like beans. We had beans for breakfast, beans for lunch, and beans for supper. I was hungry all the time! So committing to an occasional day of increased hunger was quite a challenge for me. But we felt called to fast and pray for our ministry there, and we determined to stick to our commitment.

One weekend, we were invited to work in the kitchen during a women's retreat for all English-speaking missionary women in Costa Rica. We were so excited because this meant that for one weekend our weary brains and tongues could speak in English! We desperately needed some encouragement at that time and though we would be working, we knew that there would be enough down-time to fellowship with the other missionary women. There was just one problem. The weekend fell during our monthly fast. Did I mention that we would be working in the kitchen? Did I mention that this would be American food? Did I mention that beans were not on the menu? Did I mention that I felt hungry all the time?

In the scope of life's great problems, this was small. But my stomach did not think so. I have never experienced greater temptation toward food as I did when I was preparing and serving that savory, sweet-smelling American meal to those ladies. I purposely breathed deeply through my nose as I carried the plates, in order to at least enjoy the smell of the food. Only that made it worse. My stomach growled, my body and spirit felt weak. I had the typical war in my mind: God would surely understand. He knows how much I need this comfort of familiar food. I am not a legalistic person. I know about His grace. But though the thoughts were true, I was at that time using them to justify what I wanted to do. Though it may not have been "sinful" for me to break the fast, I would have missed out on a great blessing.

We survived the fast, and the next morning it was time to break the fast. Most of the women had returned to their homes and there were only about eight of us left. One of the other women prepared the best breakfast that I have ever had: eggs, bacon, homemade biscuits and muffins, fresh fruit, and—best of all—not a bean in sight!

The Feast

Like Hannah experienced, the hunger made the feast all the better! Our longings are like that. At the end of our longing (and the end will eventually come) our spiritual eyes are sharpened and our appreciation for the simple blessings is increased. And the spiritual feast that finally comes is all the more wonderful and fulfilling because of the time of longing.

"She who was barren has borne seven children..." (I Sam. 2:5). Now I don't know how many children Hannah went on to have, but at that point, she couldn't have had seven because Samuel, her first born, was only three or four years old. Remember that the number seven stands for completion and perfection. Hannah was saying that God Himself had completed her, and His plans were perfect.

> *"The LORD brings death and makes alive;*
> *he brings down to the grave and raises up.*
> *The LORD sends poverty and wealth;*
> *he humbles and he exalts.*
> *He raises the poor from the dust*
> *and lifts the needy from the ash heap;*
> *he seats them with princes*
> *and has them inherit a throne of honor.*
> *"For the foundations of the earth are the LORD's;*
> *upon them he has set the world.*
> *He will guard the feet of his saints,*
> *but the wicked will be silenced in darkness.*
> *"It is not by strength that one prevails;*
> *those who oppose the LORD will be shattered.*
> *He will thunder against them from heaven;*
> *the LORD will judge the ends of the earth.*
> *"He will give strength to his king*
> *and exalt the horn of his anointed."*
>
> (I Samuel 2:6-10)

"The Lord brings death and makes alive; he brings down to the grave and raises up" (I Sam. 2:6). Jesus is the resurrection and the life. When we surrender to Him, die to ourselves and our own plans, He makes a new and wonderful creation out of our lives, our souls, and our circumstances. Hannah basically was saying she had been to hell and back, and knew that her God was the God of Resurrection!

"He lifts the needy from the ash heap; he seats them with princes and has them inherit a throne of honor" (I Sam. 2:7). Hannah was treated like a homeless person taken from her bed of trash and placed in a castle with royalty, seated in the place of honor. That is what He wants to do for each of us.

"It is not by strength that one prevails..." (I Sam. 2:9). It is in the Lord's strength that we prevail. We are not strong enough in our own strength. We will not find the inner strength to endure trials if our inner being has not found Christ. It is the Spirit of the living God which lives within us that gives us strength. *"Not by might, not by power, but by my Spirit says the Lord"* (Zech. 4:6). His strength in our weakness brings glory to the Lord.

"My mouth boasts over my enemies, for I delight in your deliverance" (1Sam. 2:1). Hannah's mouth of praise silenced her enemies; not only the other wife, but also the ultimate enemy, Satan. Her very life proved them wrong. The opposite of what they said proved to be true.

Let's look back at the beginning of our story. 1Samuel 1:19

says, *"Early the next morning they arose and worshiped before the LORD and then went back to their home at Ramah. Elkanah lay with Hannah his wife, and the LORD remembered her."* They said she was forgotten by God, but the Lord remembered her!

Time would prove the extent of His favor. This child for whom she had prayed was indeed one of the most honored and devoted and vital ministers of God in the history of the prophets. We don't even hear of the other children of Elkanah. Hannah found that *"There is no one holy like the Lord... there is no Rock like our God"* (1Sam. 2:2). The Lord Himself was her Stone of Remembrance. She not only received a new son, but also a new set of spiritual eyes. Her perspective was changed, allowing her to see clearly the mighty plans that God had for her.

Perspective

The trick to seeing God work in miraculous ways in our longings, even if the miraculous is wrapped up in the ordinary, is perspective. We must remember to keep our eyes focused on the perspective of God. Our carnal nature (our pre-Jesus self) is not able to see things in the same way that our post-Jesus self can. And unfortunately, that old carnal nature keeps creeping up on us throughout our lives.

It takes an effort on our part to have eyes that see things from a godly perspective. I remember during my junior year in high school, I went to spend spring break with my grandmother in Clarksdale, Mississippi. During that visit, I went with her to her weekly Bible study at the First Baptist Church. Twenty-plus years later, I still remember what the pastor taught that day. The Holy Spirit anointed his teaching as he taught from the passage in Romans 12, about being offered as a living sacrifice:

"I urge you therefore, brethren, by the mercies of God, to present your bodies a living and holy sacrifice, acceptable to God, which is your spiritual service of worship. And do not be conformed to this world, but be transformed by the renewing of your mind, that you may prove what the will of God is, that which is good and acceptable and perfect."
(Romans 12:1-2; NAS)

The pastor said that offering ourselves as a living sacrifice involves a daily offering to the Lord. So for all these years I have frequently prayed, "Lord, take my eyes this day that I may see people and situations as you see them. Take my hands this day that I may love and help people that you put in my path. Take my feet this day that I may walk in your ways, and that everywhere I go, I may glorify you. Take my mind this day, that I will have your thoughts and your perspective. Take my heart this day that I may be completely and wholly committed to you."

And what is the result of offering ourselves as a living sacrifice on a daily basis? First of all, as we find in the Roman's passage, we are giving to God a holy and acceptable act of worship. We are honoring Him and pleasing Him. And secondly, we are able to be transformed by the renewing of our minds. We are able to see our situations from a godly perspective. We are not conformed to the standards of this world. We are able to stand up and be counted as God-followers because our lives are different; our lives now reflect the image of Jesus, because our carnal nature is pushed aside so that His light shines through us. And it is at this point that we are able to see the good and acceptable and perfect will of God. How merciful our God is to show us this guide for changing our perspective.

The Window

Years later, I learned even more about perspective in an unlikely place. When we were living in Costa Rica, Kelli and I caught a bus each Saturday morning to a refugee camp called Los Guidos. Los Guidos consisted of hundreds of makeshift, dirt-floored houses, built of scraps of wood or pieces of tin. Basically, they were simple shelters from the daily rain. Over several months we began to develop friendships with the children, many of whom waited faithfully each Saturday for our bus to arrive. One of these faithful children was a 12-year-old boy named Enrique. Enrique attended our Bible school each week regardless of which sector we were scheduled.

One Saturday after Bible school, Enrique invited us to walk to his house to meet his family. We agreed to go, and he joyfully led us on the dirt road to his house. When we arrived, we saw a one-room shack, built up on stilts to avoid the mudslides of the embankment on which it was built. We climbed the muddy hill to get to the entrance, thankful that we had chosen to wear our hiking boots that day.

When we entered his home, we were greeted by his mother, father, and three siblings, all who lived together in the one-room home. The home was mostly empty, except for a worn sofa and a few other belongings in the corner of the room. There was one big "window" on the back wall of the home which was simply a big rectangle cut out of the plywood wall. The window had no glass, and I just assumed that they must cover the space with a piece of cloth or plastic when the rains came.

Enrique was obviously very excited to have us as guests in his home. The rest of the family greeted us with sincere hospitality, and we were amazed at the joy exuding from their home, despite their obvious poor conditions. I could tell that Enrique was anxious and excited to show us something, although I could not see what that could be considering the sparseness of the room. We followed him over to the back wall where the opening was cut for the window. With a grand sweeping motion he presented the object of his excitement. What he was so anxious to show us was the view of the mountains which could be seen from the opening. It was breathtaking! We all stood for several minutes taking in the scene, pausing to focus on the beautiful details which Enrique obviously considered his own precious treasure.

My life was changed that day. I began to see things differently with Enrique's perspective. Enrique did not focus on what he did not have. Enrique focused on the great blessings that had so richly been bestowed upon him. He lived out a great truth: contentment is not getting what we want, but rather realizing what we have. Enrique had learned what Paul meant when he wrote to the Philippians about being content:

> "...for I have learned to be content whatever the circumstances. I know what it is to be in need, and I know what it is to have plenty. I have learned the secret of being content in any and every situation, whether well fed or hungry, whether living in plenty or in want. I can do everything through him who gives me strength."
>
> (Philippians 4:11-13)

The Fullness of the Glory

This contentment involves a trust in the holy and all-powerful Father. It is a trust in the love of God. And when we get a glimpse of the fullness of that love, it prompts us to want to follow Him no matter what the cost. We want to be godly, not because of a set of legalistic rules, but because we have seen His love and grace and are overwhelmed by it. In his first letter to Timothy, Paul wrote: *"But godliness with contentment is great gain. For we brought nothing into the world, and we can take nothing out of it"* (1Tim. 6:6-7).

We can't gain that contentment by constantly looking at our circumstances and ourselves, because even the best circumstances have flaws if the focus remains long enough. Rather than spending our time, energy, dreams, and focus on the aspects of life that will always be imperfect, let's turn the focus to what is always perfect—the Creator, the Giver of Life, the Author and Perfector of our faith; the All-Knowing, All-Understanding, All-Encompassing King of Kings and Lord of Lords.

There is a window in the life of every person which screams to be noticed; a window which reveals the blessings from the One who loves us perfectly; a window into the heart and soul of God. The fact that He wants to provide that window for us to see is a miracle in itself. If we remember to look out God's window, we will see that there is a lot more going on than we realize. He is working all things together for our good and His glory. We are privileged to play even a small part in His holy plan.

Our ordinary friend, Joshua, had a faithful heart because he recognized the miracles and remembered them even when the others forgot. And the same God, our Father, who does not change like shifting shadows, wants to work in extraordinary, miraculous ways in our ordinary lives. But we need the right perspective to see His hand move.

Even if our thoughts are unholy, we can offer them to Him and ask Him to give us eyes to see situations and people the way He sees them. So, I think it is OK to ask why God let the longing go on for so long in Hannah's life. Perhaps she needed that length of time to come to complete surrender. We will see at the end of her story that His answer would require sacrifice on her part so that the fullness of the glory of the Lord in the midst of the answer would be revealed. The longer we have to wait, the more impossible in our own strength the surrender is, the greater the glory to God.

How did Hannah's story end?
- Hannah's son, Samuel, heard the audible voice of God during a time when God had been silent for generations.
- Two books of the Bible are designated to his name and life history.
- He was used of God to listen, select and anoint David as king.
- He was used to speak God's truth to all the people.
- He was wise beyond his years.
- He became the first judge of Israel.
- His sons became judges, which showed generational favor.
- Kings consulted his advice. He was actually more powererful than the king.
- He set up an Ebenezer: his own stone of remembrance.

Like his mother, he found that *"There is no one holy like the Lord; there is no one besides you; there is no Rock like our God"* (1Sam. 2:2).

Stones
of
Listening
Choice & Love
Displayed

Chapter 6
Listening for the
Footsteps of Jesus

One of the first things we learn about the boy Samuel is that he was a good listener. He listened to God even when he didn't understand.

"The boy Samuel ministered before the Lord under Eli. In those days the word of the Lord was rare; there were not many visions. One night Eli, whose eyes were becoming so weak that he could barely see, was lying down in his usual place. The lamp of God had not yet gone out, and Samuel was lying down in the temple of the Lord, where the ark of God was. Then the Lord called Samuel. Samuel answered, 'Here I am.' And he ran to Eli and said, 'Here I am; you called me.' But Eli said, 'I did not call; go back and lie down.' So he went and lay down. Again, the Lord called, 'Samuel!' And Samuel got up and went to Eli and said, 'Here I am; you called me.' 'My son,' Eli said, 'I did not call; go back and lie down.' Now Samuel did not yet know the Lord: The word of the Lord had not yet been revealed to

him. The Lord called Samuel a third time, and Samuel got up and went to Eli and said, 'Here I am; you called me.' Then Eli realized that the Lord was calling the boy. So Eli told Samuel, 'Go and lie down, and if he calls you, say, 'Speak, Lord, for your servant is listening.' So Samuel went and lay down in his place. The Lord came and stood there, calling as at the other times, 'Samuel, Samuel!' Then Samuel said, 'Speak, for your servant is listening.'"

(1Samuel 3:1-10)

If we learn to listen to Him, we will hear Him speak to us. Maybe not audible, because we might die from the shock! But in our spirits, we can hear Him whisper to us, calling us by name. We must live a surrendered life, which causes us to daily say, "Speak, for your servant is listening". And, He will speak to us through His Word, through the still, small voice of the Holy Spirit, and even through our circumstances.

Yani was a wife, mother of three, English teacher, native Costa Rican. Yani was my friend. I met Yani while working at a Christian school in Costa Rica. She invited my friend, Kelli, and me into her home when we were lonely and homesick, young and single girls living in a foreign land. She made us feel that we were part of her family when we were so in need of family, despite the age, language, and cultural differences. Yani spoke to us as friends, and was there to lovingly teach us the ways of a foreign country.

Often, Yani invited us to her home for "coffee". This coffee time included sandwiches and sweets, "pan dulce or tres leches," and of course, the strong, hot coffee, which she desperately craved by three o'clock in the afternoon. We could only stomach her coffee with lots and lots of "leche y azuchar, por favor!" (Milk and sugar, please!). It was during these coffee times that she often opened up her heart with tales of her childhood, dreams for her future and the future of her children, and of her faith in God.

She spoke in English, which was a welcome reprieve from the constant struggle to comprehend this beautiful, but foreign language. Though her English was very good, her accent was different enough that we had to listen intently in order to understand what she was saying. We listened intently not only to understand, but also because we loved her, and we knew that she loved us.

One day, at coffee time, Yani shared an experience from her life, the memory of which was still both painful and precious. She shared of when her daughter became very ill. They rushed her to the hospital and spent a long, difficult night not knowing what the outcome would be. At one point during the night, a compassionate Christian nurse felt compelled to pray with Yani. The words of her prayer were simple: that God would make His presence known to Yani and her family, and that He would heal her daughter.

Yani struggled to describe in English the depth of peace that she felt at the moment of that prayer. In heavily accented English she said, "When that nurse prayed ... I could ... I could hear the footsteps of Jesus."

The footsteps of Jesus! If we listen, they are all around us, walking before us, with us and behind us.

The footsteps of Jesus assure us that yes, He is here as Wonderful Counselor, Mighty God, the Prince of Peace and there'll

the wholeness He brings. But we must remember
_ally and intently, not only to understand, but be-
_use we love Him, and we know that He really loves us! Listen
for His footsteps and you will surely hear.

Psalm 46:10 says, *"Be still, and know that I am God!"* (NLT).
The New American Standard translation says it this way: *"Cease
striving and know that I am God."* And that is the invitation for you
this day: Sit down, be still before the Lord, and listen to Him.
Cease all of your striving and know that He is God, the extraordinary, awesome God who is pleased to speak to ordinary souls.

Chapter 7
Choose What Is Better

Many other godly examples in Scripture reaffirm our need to listen to God. One of the best examples is found in the familiar story of Mary and Martha. I can relate to the story of Mary and Martha because we live in a "Martha world". We all tend to push, push, push and strive, strive, strive—ever hurrying faster. Many of us live a "microwave" existence, which ultimately creates strife and stress. Our generation has lost any form or concept of "Sabbath rest". Not the legalistic Sabbath rest that Jesus rejected, but the Sabbath rest that causes us to stop from our ways to think and reflect and act upon His ways.

The Sabbath rest which my soul needs and craves is a daily need, not just a go-to-church-on-Sunday need. It is a letting go of all that I strive for, to be renewed and refreshed and strengthened to grasp everything that He strives and desires for me. And without some Sabbath rest on our part, we don't have the ability to really listen and be still and know that He is God. As I recently studied the story of Mary and Martha again, I found

ghts for my soul. I found a model of listening and a
_ure to listen. See if you find it, too:

"As Jesus and his disciples were on their way, he came to a
village where a woman named Martha opened her home
to him. She had a sister called Mary, who sat at the Lord's feet listen-
ing to what he said. But Martha was distracted by all the prepara-
tions that had to be made. She came to him and asked, 'Lord, don't
you care that my sister has left me to do the work by myself? Tell her
to help me!'

"'Martha, Martha,' the Lord answered, 'you are worried and
upset about many things, but only one thing is needed. Mary has chosen
what is better, and it will not be taken away from her.'"

(Luke 10:38-42)

Martha was a doer. She had her list of things to do and was
being very efficient in doing them. There was just one problem. Martha was caught up in the "tyranny of the urgent". She
started out great. She was the one who opened her home to
Jesus, but maybe she had not learned to fully open her heart to
Him. It was not that what she was doing was not important, or
even necessary, but she was missing the moment.

I believe that if Martha had stopped to listen to Jesus, she
would have had the joy of experiencing God's Word being true.
For His Word says in Matthew 6:33: *"Seek first his kingdom and his*
righteousness, and all these things will be given to you as well." So many
times, God has proven Himself to me. For when I take time to
first seek Him, I find that my time seems to multiply, and I am

able to accomplish all the other necessary things as well.

From Mary's part of this story we learn to Stop, Look, and Listen. That is what we teach our children to buffer their threat of danger in crossing the road. That will also help buffer the many threats that Satan sends our way. Remember to place first things first. We all desperately need to daily sit at the feet of Jesus. Thinking of the position evokes the perfect picture of humility and trust. It is humbling to sit at someone's feet, even if it is only figuratively. It is acknowledging a need in us and that we do not have all the answers, nor do we have it all together.

So much of our striving is to convince the world, and maybe even ourselves, that we have it all together; that we are adequate in every way. What freedom we find when we admit to ourselves that we don't have it all together. What intimacy we find in friendships when we admit to others our inadequacies. When we sit at the feet of Jesus we truly are choosing what is better, and we will be blessed for it. God will agree with us that we don't have it all together, and that yes, indeed, we are inadequate. But in that recognition, God will shower us with His grace and mercy. Scripture promises that He will lift us from the pit and place us on solid Rock, the only sure foundation. And He will speak words of love, encouragement, and acceptance and adoration. Did you know that you are adored by the Creator of the Universe, the King of all Kings? That knowledge is almost too much to comprehend. And you are adored because He loves you, not because of all of your "strivings".

From Martha we learn: Don't be so busy doing necessary things that we miss the most important things. Sometimes less is more. Being distracted makes us miss the most important things. Not listening to God leads often to self-centeredness and a "pity party". Sitting at the feet of Jesus on a daily basis is a great vaccine for those emotions.

Deep down I must admit that often when I have read this story I have thought, *Well, Martha did have a point. She was doing all the work. Food had to be prepared.* But this time I thought about Martha and Jesus' response to her:

> *"'Martha, Martha,' the Lord answered, 'you are worried and upset about many things, but only one thing is needed. Mary has chosen what is better, and it will not be taken away from her.'"* (Luke 10:41-42)

He spoke to her almost as we would speak to a child that we love who doesn't understand. And I thought for the first time of what Jesus might have been thinking, but didn't say...

- Martha, Martha, don't you see that our time together on this earth is short? Do you not see that you need this quiet time with me so that you will be prepared to endure what lies ahead?
- Martha, Martha, don't you know yet Who I am and what I can do? Remember the 5,000 hungry people, Martha? Remember how I used the five loaves and two fish and everyone left full, with plenty of leftovers for later? Don't you know that I could have done the same thing for you today?

When my friend Kelli and I went to do mission work in Costa Rica for six months, our primary mission was to teach English in a Costa Rican school; but our true mission turned out to be our work on Saturdays in Los Guidos. There we would simply show up with a Bible lesson and a craft, and go from door to door inviting the children to join us. We met under a large tree in the center of the camp. As I have said, the homes there consisted of pieces of wood or tin thrown together to make dirt floor shacks. The children were very poor and often hungry and dirty.

One day in particular, God revealed His grace, mercy and power in an awesome way. We had been going every Saturday for a couple of months and we had never had over 15 children. As we packed the bag of supplies, I carefully counted out enough supplies for 20 craft projects, just in case we had a couple of extra children. To our surprise, as we began the lesson with singing and a Bible story, the children kept coming and coming. I began to feel very nervous about the craft projects, knowing that that was the biggest reason that they were coming, since this was a luxury that was uncommon to those children. As soon as I finished counting, more children would come.

I began to pray furiously as our translator finished up the story. At last count I realized that there were 40 children gathered around the big tree listening to a story of God's faithfulness. I didn't know what else to do except to pass out the supplies. I reached into the bag to gather supplies, Kelli reached into the bag to gather supplies, and Ivonnia, our translator, reached into the bag to gather supplies. We kept going back to the bag for more supplies over and over until every child had made a craft project. After the children left, I looked into the bag once again—there were still supplies in the bag! I had packed the bag myself. I knew exactly what was in the bag. I wept when I realized in my heart that our Lord is the same yesterday, today and forever. The same Lord, who blessed and multiplied the fish and the loaves, multiplied our supplies that day. And though those 40 children will never know of the miracle that day, I will never forget. How often does God perform miracles in the day-to-day lives of His children which are never even realized? I believe it is more often than we think!

to agony and death? He went to see his dear friends, Mary and Martha and Lazarus. Despite their lack of understanding and lack of faith, Jesus counted them as friends. But He had a lot of friends. Many people would have, at that point, gladly welcomed Him into their homes.

Why did He want to spend His last days with them? Think about where you would want to go if you knew you were about to die. You would go where you knew you were loved. Jesus went where He would be loved extravagantly. And that extravagant love would usher in the resurrection power of the risen Christ.

> "Six days before the Passover, Jesus arrived at Bethany, where Lazarus lived, whom Jesus had raised from the dead. Here a dinner was given in Jesus' honor. Martha served, while Lazarus was among those reclining at the table with him. Then Mary took about a pint of pure nard, an expensive perfume; she poured it on Jesus' feet and wiped his feet with her hair. And the house was filled with the fragrance of the perfume. But one of his disciples, Judas Iscariot, who was later to betray him, objected, 'Why wasn't this perfume sold and the money given to the poor? It was worth a year's wages.' He did not say this because he cared about the poor but because he was a thief; as keeper of the money bag, he used to help himself to what was put into it. 'Leave her alone,' Jesus replied. 'It was intended that she should save this perfume for the day of my burial. You will always have the poor among you, but you will not always have me.'"
>
> (John 12: 1-12)

Looking at the above passage, we must ask ourselves what

this extravagant love looks like. First of all, they showed their love for Jesus by welcoming and honoring Him. It was all about Him. Martha was still being Martha by serving, yet it appears that she was now using her giftedness to honor Him and serve Him, rather than to recruit any praise or admiration for her like she had done before.

Love Displayed

After one of our Saturday Bible schools in Los Guidos, Costa Rica, we found ourselves in the home of a precious Costa Rican lady named Alicia. When she walked with her children to the great tree in the center of sector eight, where we held our weekly program, she pulled me aside to invite us to come to her house after Bible school. We gladly accepted the invitation, although I must confess that I was a bit nervous. We did not know the lady very well, and at that point we had never been invited to enter any of the dilapidated shacks which covered the mountainside.

As soon as all of the other children had walked back to their homes, we walked to Alicia's home with her three children. My eyes had to adjust a bit when we first entered the dirt-floor dwelling. There was no electricity, so the only light was from the doorway, and from a "window" which had been cut from the tin and wood-scrap walls. The home was just one room which was partitioned by sheets hanging across a rope attached to the ceiling.

Alicia excitedly welcomed us to her home. I noticed that the dirt floor had been neatly swept and all of her meager belongings were in order. On the table, I noticed several broken glasses from several different patterns, a small plate full of saltine crackers, and a chipped pitcher of lemonade. There were no chairs for us to sit, so we simply stood around the table and listened while she talked of her life and her love for the Lord. Such sweet fellowship of believers we experienced that day! She offered us the crackers and lemonade, which we received with a gratitude that had nothing to do with what was offered. I was overcome with her pure hospitality. Although we had been repeatedly warned against eating or drinking in that area, I took what was offered and silently prayed the prayer that my missionary friend, Ben Pierce, had once shared with me: "Lord, I'll get it down, if You keep it down!"

When we were thanking her for her invitation and hospitality, she joyfully responded, "Este es mi fiesta!" "This is my party!" a party given in honor of us; a party given with grace and elegance despite the limited resources that she had to work with. Such pure hospitality and generosity I have rarely, if ever, seen since that day. And such conviction it brought to my soul. How many times do I resist reaching out to others because my house is not perfect, or my dishes don't match, or I don't have time to create an extravagant meal? And how many times do my guests leave my house feeling the joy of being honored, and the warmth of sweet fellowship.

After that day in Los Guidos, I am without excuses. I need to share my "party". The kingdom of God is a party to be shared by all that we are privileged to come in contact with. And Scripture tells us that when we do it for "the least of these," we do it unto Him. So whenever you reach out to anyone with a pure, loving heart, you are reaching up to Jesus. That shows extravagant love for Him.

In the story of Mary and Martha, we see that they displayed their love for Jesus in a number of significant ways:

One, we see that they showed their love for Jesus in the way they spent their money.

Mary and Martha did not spend their money extravagantly on fleshy, selfish gain, but on that which would honor and benefit the Lord and His kingdom. The oil that Mary used to anoint Jesus was said to have been worth a years' wages. That is extravagant love. I remember when we were in residency. Money was very tight. We had a cute little house and hand-me-down furniture, and it felt like home. For Christmas one year I got money from my parents and Mont's parents. On New Year's Day Mont and I went to an antique auction and I was able to buy at an incredible bargain eight Chippendale dining room chairs. I was so excited. I called my friend Angie right away and she was excited with me.

Soon after, we had Angie and her husband, Trey, over for dinner. During dessert, Trey leaned way back in his chair and we all heard a "Crack!" He jumped up, and we all saw that the chair was broken. Angie was mortified. When we were cleaning up, she said, "Sara, I'm so sorry about the chair! I know it is your most prized possession!" I suddenly felt sick at my stomach. What had my attitude about the chairs said to her? I quickly told her that my family and friends were my most prized possession. And I had to do business with the Lord about that later.

We waited seven years to fix that chair. In the mean time, we always assigned the lightest person to sit on it, with plenty of warning. We could have fixed it before that, but I wanted the reminder. I love to decorate. I love a pretty home and pretty clothes. But Mont and I always strive to hold it all very loosely. It all belongs to the Lord anyway, and what we are given is meant to be shared. Our happiness does not depend on the material things, and if it ever does find its way to an improper place in my heart, it soon makes me feel empty and unfulfilled. We should extravagantly love Jesus by the way we spend our money. This truly does bring blessing to our souls.

Two, we see that they showed their love for Jesus by their willingness to be misunderstood and ridiculed because of Him.

The so-called disciple, Judas, belittled and criticized the display of love that Mary showed. We should realize that it had not been made known yet who Judas was truly serving. How discouraging that must have been to have another follower rebuke her publicly. Yet, it appears that Mary was not fazed by the opinion of others. While Judas the thief, acting like the evil one he served, tried to steal her joy, Mary walked in triumph. The Lord Himself defended her. He is our mighty defender, too.

I have had the privilege of going on trips to China several times in the past few years. China is a beautiful country. It has many problems, but God is clearly working in and through the Chinese. My friend, James Loftin, says that China is the most strategically important country in the world today.

While on a trip to China in 2007, I had the privilege of discussing this same passage with a group of women that had gathered in a home. I marveled at how similar we were. We are troubled by many of the same insecurities, but there was a big difference. These Chinese sisters had made a great effort to be present in that meeting. In fact, their presence there was evidence of their great, extravagant love for Jesus. If they had been caught in an unauthorized religious meeting with a foreigner, government officials could have fined or even incarcerated them. I met a precious woman named "Mary" at that Bible Study. She is a beautiful, sweet Chinese believer who is in full-time ministry. She shared about the verbal abuse she has endured from her family, especially her mother, for being a Christian. Yet she has continued to follow Jesus with patience and joy. That is extravagant love.

I have also had the privilege of meeting with a Chinese pastor who had recently spent two-and-a-half years in a prison. His only crime was preaching the Word of God. I am not including his picture or using his real name because I don't want to do anthing that might be used to incriminate him in the future. "Brother Jacob" told us that while in prison, they were allowed only one shower a year. They worked from before dawn to about 11:30 at night assembling Christmas lights, which would be sold all over the world. Just like the ones I hang all over my house in December. My first reaction was that I didn't think I could put up Christmas lights anymore, but then I decided to use them as a reminder to pray for our persecuted brothers and sisters who are shining lights for Jesus.

Brother Jacob also shared that many miracles took place in prison. I well remember his story about a guard that had a Christian mother. In fact, the guard's mother had actually been in Brother Jacob's church. Although the guard was not a Christian, he honored his mother and snuck a Bible to the pastor. He also managed to obtain a radio. Because the pastor was such a godly and trustworthy man, the guards gave him more and more responsibilities at the prison. One of Brother Jacob's duties was cleaning the guards' locker room. So it was in the guards' locker room that he had private moments to read his Bible and listen to Christian radio programs being broadcast from countries like Korea. Brother Jacob was so hungry and desperate for the Word of God and the encouragement and comfort of the Holy Spirit, he was willing to risk extra jail time and beatings if he was caught. That is a risk that millions of believers in places like North Korea, Iran and China are willing to take. That is extravagant love.

Three, we see that they showed their love for Jesus by being willing to serve Him in humility.

Mary fell at Jesus' feet, a sign of respect and awe. And she ceremonially washed His feet, which was the job of a servant or slave. Mary wiped His feet with her hair. In those days a women's hair was her personal glory. There were specific instructions for women about their hair. When Mary let her hair down to wipe His feet she was communicating two things: She was saying, "Lord, I give all my glory to you, for you alone are worthy." And she was saying, "I don't care what others think. I am willing to appear foolish in expressing my love to my Lord." That is extravagant love.

Others, also, experienced and enjoyed the fruit of Mary's extravagant love. Note that *"the house was filled with the fragrance of the perfume"* (John 12:3). When we love Jesus in an extravagant way, the overflow of that love spreads to others. Even if they don't understand fully, there will be a positive effect for those with pure hearts. As the Scriptures say in Ephesians 5:1-2: *"Be imitators of God, therefore, as dearly loved children and live a life of love, just as Christ loved us and gave himself up for us as a fragrant offering and sacrifice to God."* Just as an adoring child imitates his father, so we can imitate Jesus by offering the sacrifice of praise to God and love to others. And this sacrifice will be wonderfully fragrant to those pure-hearted ones who witness and experience it.

Four, and perhaps most significantly, we also see that Mary anointed His feet.

In another gospel, it is said that she anointed His head. And it was more customary to anoint the head. In many passages of the Bible, we find that the head was anointed to signify a prophet, like Elijah or Elisha. And anointing of the head was especially important in anointing a king, like David or Solomon. But nothing could make Jesus more of a king. He was already King of Kings when He was lying in a manger. He was worshiped as a king by the shepherds, and the wise men brought Him kingworthy gifts.

John was possibly closer to Jesus than any other disciple, and maybe to Mary, Martha, and Lazarus indicated by the fact that He called them by name. Perhaps John, being close to the situation, was inspired to focus on the fact that she went a step further than the norm and anointed His feet, because there is unusual significance in that fact.

What needed anointing were His feet, for He had a long, painful journey ahead of Him. He had to walk the hill of Calvary.

He had to have those anointed feet nailed to a cross. But most importantly, His feet were anointed for burial, because through death, His anointed feet would fulfill the very first prophesy of the coming Messiah.

"So the Lord God said to the serpent [Satan, who had tricked Eve], 'Because you have done this, 'Cursed are you above all the livestock and all the wild animals! You will crawl on your belly and you will eat dust all the days of your life. [Here comes the first prophesy!] And I will put enmity between you and the woman, and between your offspring and hers; he [Eve's future offspring, Jesus!] will crush your head, and you will strike his heel.'"

(Genesis 3: 14; author emphasis added)

You see, Jesus would use those anointed feet to spiritually stomp Satan's headship, forever giving victory to all who believe! We will spend a lot of our time in eternity at those anointed feet, falling down at His feet, casting our crowns at His feet. Why don't we just go ahead and start loving Him extravagantly like that now, worshipping Him with all our heart and soul and mind and time and resources and homes.

After I thought all about what it looked like to love Jesus extravagantly, I had to ask myself, "Would Jesus have come to my house? Is my home; my activities, my worship, and my friendship with Him a place that shows forth extravagant love for Him?" Would He have come to your house?

It is significant that Jesus stayed in Bethany for six days. On the seventh day, He entered Jerusalem. Remember that seven is the biblical number for completion and perfection. Everything was fulfilled which needed to take place before the ultimate sacrifice began. And the last thing which needed to take place was the anointing for burial which Mary fulfilled through her extravagant display of love. Once we come to the place of surrender and extravagant love, then we are prepared to see an extraordinary God work mightily in our ordinary lives.

*Stones
of
Timing
&
The Name*

Chapter 9
For Such A Time As This

Charles Spurgeon was a powerful and famous minister whose anointed ministry began in the mid to late 1800s and the fruit of which is still seen today. Many have called him the "Prince of Preachers". At the height of his ministry, he spoke twice weekly to thousands of people at the Metropolitan Tabernacle in London. Yet, in his writings we find that he wrote:

"I sometimes think I might have been in darkness and despair until now had it not been for the goodness of God in sending a snowstorm, one Sunday morning, while I was going to a certain place of worship." i

Because of the bad weather, he entered a Primitive Methodist Chapel, joining about a dozen people in worship. He wrote that *"they sang so loudly that they made people's head ache,"* but he didn't mind, *"for I wanted to know how I might be saved, and if they could tell me that, I did not care how much they made my head ache."* ii

The regular minister did not show up that day, so a member of the small congregation got up to speak. Spurgeon described the impromptu preacher as *"a very thin-looking man, a shoemaker, or tailor, or something of that sort..."*iii (In other words, an ordinary man, someone who was an unlikely candidate for the extraordinary.) In fact, Spurgeon went on to say that this ordinary man *"was obliged to stick to his text, for the simple reason that he had little else to say."*iv

The text that substitute preacher had chosen was from Isaiah 45:22, *"Look unto me, and be ye saved, all the ends of the earth."* Spurgeon describes what happened that day in the following words:

> *"He did not even pronounce the words rightly, but that did not matter. There was, I thought, a glimpse of hope for me in that text. The preacher began thus:--'My dear friends, this is a very simple text indeed. It says, 'Look.' Now lookin' don't take a deal of pains. It ain't liftin' your foot or your finger; it is just, 'Look.' Well, a man needn't go to College to learn to look. You may be the biggest fool, and yet you can look. Anyone can look; even a child can look. But then the text says, 'Look unto to Me.' Ay!' said he is broad Essex, 'many on ye are lookin' to yourselves, but it's no use lookin' there. You'll never find any comfort in yourselves... Jesus Christ says, 'Look unto Me.'"* v

The man continued on for several minutes, until he reached the end of his sermon. Spurgeon went on to say, that suddenly, he saw...

> *"...the way of salvation. I had been waiting to do fifty things, but when I heard that work, 'Look!' what a charming word it seemed*

to me! Oh! I looked until I could almost have looked my eyes away. There and then the cloud was gone, the darkness had rolled away, and that moment I saw the sun; and I could have risen that instant, and sung with the most enthusiastic of them, of the precious blood of Christ, and the simple faith which looks alone to Him. Oh, that somebody had told me this before, 'Trust Christ, and you shall be saved.'" [vi]

The thing that I love the most about that story is that the person that led the "Prince of Preachers" to Christ was a very ordinary man. He was not a preacher, he was not very educated, but he loved Jesus. And God used that ordinary man to produce extraordinary fruit.

Queen Esther

Now I want to look at another ordinary person who was used extraordinarily by God. She was a young Jewish girl named Esther; an ordinary girl who became the Queen and helped save her people from sure destruction. It is a great historical account filled with intrigue, suspense and bravery. As I pondered this story it occurred to me that it must be of great significance because it was set apart in Scriptures from the other books.

There are many other wonderful historical accounts of various God-followers found throughout the books of the Old Testament. The histories of many of the great spiritual forefathers are compiled together in the Books of Genesis through 2 Chronicles. The stories of better known patriarchs of faith such as Noah, Abraham, Isaac, and Moses are compiled together in a conglomeration of many important historical accounts, some of which had various contributing authors. Why was this story set apart in its own book, instead of simply being added to the other great historical accounts?

The fact that the story revolves around the life of a woman makes the fact that it was set apart even more significant. This story was set in a time when women's equality and rights were unheard of. I am sure there is some important reason for it being set apart in a self-titled book, but my own contemplation believes that it is because its message was so important that it did not need to be lost among the numerous other stories. While not more important than the story of our other patriarchs of faith, it must have a message within, historically as well as practically, that merits a pause, a reflection, a remembrance.

My NIV Study Bible states that *"The author's central purpose was to record the institution of the annual festival of Purim and to keep alive for later generations the memory of the great deliverance of the Jewish people during the reign of Xerxes."* vii Basically, the author of this book had a stone of remembrance to share. Although we do not know who wrote the book of Esther, a study of the story clearly indicates that he was a Jew. He shows great patriotism for his people in his description of the story, and it is obvious that he was not from Judah or Jerusalem but was a resident of one of the Persian cities. So our conclusion about the author might be that he, homesick for his homeland, had a desire to preserve the historical and spiritual implications of this event for the sake of patriotism to his people, and for the sake of his children and grandchildren and even those afar off.

I grew up in a small town in Mississippi which has a significant historical past. The town thrives on its history. Why is it important to remember such things, devoting years of study recalling historical accounts? I believe it is because in looking back we discover pieces of ourselves. History always shows us things that we want to hold on to and things that we can learn from the mistakes that were previously made. And, I believe it is through history that we find the common thread of the faithfulness of our Creator, weaving a tapestry that we are included in as we live out our lives. A significant fact of the Book of Esther is that it is the one book of the entire Bible that makes no mention of God. There is no doubt, however, that evidence of God as sovereign and active deity is woven throughout the story. And the story clearly shows that Esther had a deep, abiding, personal faith, which affected both her actions and the outcome within the story.

Saul and the Amalekites

To truly understand the story of Esther, we must go further back in history to a time that God gave a very specific instruction to King Saul. This instruction, found in 1Samuel 15, was that he was to lead the Israelites in battle and that, with God's help, they were to completely destroy the evil people called the Amalekites. The instructions were so explicit that they could not confuse the purpose of the battle. They were to totally obliterate the Amalekites, allowing no one to live. They were also to leave all of the riches and spoils alone, taking none for themselves as was the usual custom. God did not want them to have anything to do with any of the Amalekites or their possessions, and He made that very clear.

Now, King Saul was obedient to an extent. He led the people

in battle against the Amalekites, and as God promised, they won. However, he did not follow the instructions fully and made the decision to leave a few of the Amalekites alive, taking them as slaves. He also disobeyed God when he allowed the people to take, and keep, various riches and spoils of the war. God spoke to Samuel, Hannah's son, about Saul's disobedience. Samuel nobly confronted Saul about his lack of complete obedience. And Saul responded much like we all do when first confronted with sin…he rationalized.

"When Samuel reached him, Saul said, 'The LORD bless you! I have carried out the LORD's instructions.' But Samuel said, 'What then is this bleating of sheep in my ears? What is this lowing of cattle that I hear?'
Saul answered, 'The soldiers brought them from the Amalekites; they spared the best of the sheep and cattle to sacrifice to the LORD your God, but we totally destroyed the rest.'

"'Stop!' Samuel said to Saul. 'Let me tell you what the LORD said to me last night.' 'Tell me,' Saul replied.

"Samuel said, 'Although you were once small in your own eyes, did you not become the head of the tribes of Israel? The LORD anointed you king over Israel. And he sent you on a mission, saying, 'Go and completely destroy those wicked people, the Amalekites; make war on them until you have wiped them out.' Why did you not obey the LORD? Why did you pounce on the plunder and do evil in the eyes of the LORD?'

"'But I did obey the LORD,' Saul said. 'I went on the
LORD assigned me. I completely destroyed the Amalek
brought back Agag their king. The soldiers took sheep and cattle from
the plunder, the best of what was devoted to God, in order to sacrifice
them to the LORD your God at Gilgal.'

"But Samuel replied:
'Does the LORD delight in burnt offerings and sacrifices
as much as in obeying the voice of the LORD?
To obey is better than sacrifice,
and to heed is better than the fat of rams.'" (1Samuel 15:13-22)

Saul did not obey completely. I like to think of it like cook-
ing chicken or pork. "Almost" done will still make you very sick!
Saul did just enough right to try to justify his actions. And he assigned some of the plunder to go to God to make him feel better. But God does not need our token acknowledgements. He
sees right through that. We may fool many people, but we can't
fool God. Being completely honest with God and with you is
one of the first steps to being prepared for God's extraordinary
plan.

God demands complete obedience, not because He is a
dictator-type God, but because only He can see past, present and
future. Only He can look behind and ahead and trace the thread
of our actions in the tapestry of our life story, and the story of
the generations to come. Now, I have to stop for a moment and
remind you that this is not a call to legalism. Jesus reprimanded
the legalistic Pharisees much more than the overt sinners.

Always remember the principles of God's Grace: we don't

deserve it; we can't earn it; Jesus bought it for us; It's free! But once we experience God's grace first hand, we want with all of our hearts to please Him and show Him how much we love Him. He is a holy God who can't dwell with sin. That's why we turn to Him to set us free from sin, and to give us the power to live a life pleasing to Him. It is His grace that also shows us our sin, so that we can be relieved of it and released from it.

He does sometimes allow consequences for our sins, even consequences that are revealed further down the road. The consequences that Saul faced were both immediate and far reaching. God removed His favor from Saul and eventually replaced him with King David, who, though not perfect, yet, nonetheless, was a man after God's own heart. And it was through King David that God's ultimate plan of salvation was fulfilled when generations later Jesus was born in the lineage of David.

I believe the difference that we see between these two examples of sinful people is the heart with which they faced their sin. In Saul's story, he never really received a mighty redemption. David, on the other hand, turned his whole heart to God, acknowledged and truly repented of his sin—not just because he was caught, but because he was convicted and grieved by what he had done.

The full repercussions of the sin of King Saul were not seen immediately. However, years down the road, the ancestors of those Amalekites that were left alive caused great problems for the people of God. The Israelites were eventually taken captive from Jerusalem and carried into exile in Persia.

Chapter 10
Scenes from the Life of Esther

If Esther's life were a stage play, there would be 12 key scenes that trace the development of her story:

Scene 1: What a party!

The story of Esther begins in the setting of a great feast. King Xerxes was having a grand banquet for all of his nobles, officials, military leaders, princes, and other dignitaries from the surrounding provinces. The banquet was in celebration of his great successes, and it lasted for seven full days. Wine was flowing freely, and the king had instructed the wine stewards to serve each man whatever he wished. Queen Vashti, the wife of King Xerxes, was at the same time giving a banquet for the royal women. On the seventh day, when King Xerxes was in high spirits from wine, he commanded that Queen Vashti be brought before him in order to display her beauty to the nobles present, for she was very lovely to look at.

Scene 2: *Who does she think she is?*

However, Queen Vashti refused to come. The king was furious because she had disgraced him in front of the dignitaries. You see, at that time, a wife was more like a piece of property. Legally, she had no right to refuse to come. So the king consulted experts in matters of law and justice and it was decided that Queen Vashti would have to give up her crown and be banished from the King's presence. This was announced throughout the land as an example for the other women.

All of this was fine, until later when the king's anger had cooled and he began to miss his wife. So, to cheer the king, his attendants suggested a royal beauty pageant. The king appointed commissioners from all over the province to find the prettiest virgins to bring to the palace for a year of beauty treatments. At this point, Esther steps into the scene.

> *"Now there was in the citadel of Susa a Jew of the tribe of Benjamin, named Mordecai son of Jair, the son of Shimei, the son of Kish, who had been carried into exile from Jerusalem by Nebuchadnezzar king of Babylon, among those taken captive with Jehoiachin king of Judah. Mordecai had a cousin named Hadassah, whom he had brought up because she had neither father nor mother. This girl, who was also known as Esther, was lovely in form and features, and Mordecai had taken her as his own daughter when her father and mother died."* (Esther 2:5-7)

Scene 3: *And who are your parents?*

When we first meet Esther, we immediately see that she has

several strikes against her. She had a heritage of slavery. She was a foreigner in the land. She was an orphan. But we also see that Esther was a beautiful, young Jewish girl who had been raised by her cousin, Mordecai, after her parents had been killed. Mordecai had been carried into exile, but eventually worked his way into some sort of official role in the king's court. So, Mordecai arranged for the beautiful Esther to be one of the contestants in the royal beauty pageant. It is unclear whether Esther wanted to do this, but she obediently followed Mordecai's instructions, including keeping hidden the fact that she was Jewish.

> *"Esther had not revealed her nationality and family background, because Mordecai had forbidden her to do so. Every day he walked back and forth near the courtyard of the harem to find out how Esther was and what was happening to her. Before a girl's turn came to go in to King Xerxes, she had to complete twelve months of beauty treatments prescribed for the women, six months with oil of myrrh and six with perfumes and cosmetics."*
>
> (Esther 2:10-12)

One thing that I noticed in those verses was that Esther was humble enough to listen to godly, wise counsel. Mordecai obviously cared for Esther and he cared greatly about completely following God's way. I believe that God will send people into our lives to speak godly wisdom and wise counsel, and to encourage us in our journey to God's extraordinary plan for our lives. But we must be humble enough to listen.

Once, I had a dream. I have always dreamed vividly. My old

roommate, Kelli, called it "story time" in the mornings when I would tell her what I dreamed. I don't remember all my dreams, but I remember this one. In my dream, a ferocious lion was chasing me. I was ahead of him, but I could feel him catching up, and I was getting very tired of running. Then I ran into a big arena, and when I entered the arena suddenly people started cheering. I looked up and realized that they were cheering for me! The more I looked, the more people I recognized—family members, people from my church, friends. They were all cheering for me. Shortly after that, I read Hebrews 12:1-3:

> *"Therefore, since we are surrounded by such a great cloud of witnesses, let us throw off everything that hinders and the sin that so easily entangles, and let us run with perseverance the race marked out for us. Let us fix our eyes on Jesus, the author and perfecter of our faith, who for the joy set before Him endured the cross, scorning its shame, and sat down at the right hand of the throne of God. Consider Him who endured such opposition from sinful men, so that you will not grow weary and lose heart."*

Suddenly that verse made sense to me. God will provide a great cloud of witnesses for each of us, to cheer us on and encourage us during our lives. 1Peter 5:8 says, *"Stay alert! Watch out for your great enemy, the devil. He prowls around like a roaring lion, looking for someone to devour."* God will provide this cloud of witnesses to strengthen our faith so that we will not be devoured. But most of all, He will give us Himself, a very present help in time of need.

Scene 4: *Win him over!*

Esther won the favor of the man in charge of the new harem and he immediately provided her with beauty treatments and special food. He provided her with seven maids and moved them into the best place in the harem. We don't really know if each candidate had seven maids, but I think the Scripture tends to suggest that they did not. Remember that the number seven means completion and perfection. When God begins to prepare you for His extraordinary plan for your life, He will send you everything you need to complete you and perfect you and make you ready for extraordinary fruitfulness. But, once again, you must be humble enough to receive all the things He sends your way for preparation.

Scene 5: *Don't forget your beauty rest!*

Every day Mordecai walked back and forth near the courtyard where Esther was staying in order to find out how she was doing. For twelve months it was a continual spa experience. The girls were prescribed beauty treatments: six months with oil of myrrh and six months with perfumes and cosmetics. After the twelve months, each girl was presented to the king. The girls were allowed to take anything from the harem with them in order to entice the favor of the king. When it was Esther's turn to be presented to the king, she went before him simply adorned, taking nothing with her except what was suggested by the man in charge. She did not try to be something that she was not. She simply trusted that her ordinary life was in the hands of an extraordinary God.

Scene 6: Victory!

Esther won the favor of everyone who saw her, including the king. She basically won the beauty pageant, a royal crown was placed on her head and she became queen in place of Vashti. The king once again gave a royal banquet to celebrate his new queen! Queen Esther was now far above Mordecai in social standing and importance, but she continued to show him a father-figure respect. She did not forget her "ordinary" status. They kept in close contact through a maid, and Mordecai continued to sit at the king's gate keeping tabs on his beloved Esther. One day, while sitting at the gate, Mordecai overheard a plot to assassinate King Xerxes. He immediately told Queen Esther, who in turn reported it to the king, giving credit to Mordecai. And this incident was reported in the book of the annals, or royal history books.

Scene 7: The sins of the forefathers.

Now go back in time to King Saul's day. Remember, the people disobeyed God, and allowed some of the Amalekites to live. One of the nobles of the royal court of King Xerxes was a man named Haman.

> "After these events, King Xerxes honored Haman son of Hammedatha, the Agagite, elevating him and giving him a seat of honor higher than that of all the other nobles. All the royal officials at the king's gate knelt down and paid honor to Haman, for the king had commanded this concerning him. But Mordecai would not kneel down or pay him honor.

"Then the royal officials at the king's gate asked Mordecai, 'Why do you disobey the king's command?' Day after day they spoke to him but he refused to comply. Therefore they told Haman about it to see whether Mordecai's behavior would be tolerated, for he had told them he was a Jew.

"When Haman saw that Mordecai would not kneel down or pay him honor, he was enraged. Yet having learned who Mordecai's people were, he scorned the idea of killing only Mordecai. Instead Haman looked for a way to destroy all Mordecai's people, the Jews, throughout the whole kingdom of Xerxes." (Esther 3:1-5)

Scripture says that Haman was an Agagite. Centuries back, King Agag was the ruler of Amalek. So Agagite was another way of saying he was an Amalekite. He was a descendent of the Amalekites that had been allowed to live 500 years before. And Haman the Amalekite hated the Israelites just as much as his ancestors had. Now Haman had continued to rise in power and all the royal officials would bow as he walked by—all except Mordecai, who was determined not to bow to anyone except his God.

Scene 8: Revenge is sweet—for a season.

When Haman saw that Mordecai would not kneel down or pay him honor, he was furious. Having learned who Mordecai's people were, he began to plan a way to destroy not only Mordecai, but also the entire Jewish race. He appealed to the pride of King Xerxes, telling them of a group of people in his kingdom who did not follow the customs of the land and who did not follow the king's laws and that it was not in the king's best interest to tolerate them. Haman then suggested that a decree be issued to destroy them all.

The king agreed and plans were made for the total destruction of the Jewish people. When the Jewish people, including Mordecai, found out about the decree there was weeping and mourning throughout the land. Esther's maid came to tell her that Mordecai was in great distress; she was very worried about him. She had not heard the report yet about the planned destruction of the Jews, and she sent someone to find out what was troubling Mordecai. He sent back a copy of the edict of destruction urging her to go into the king's presence and beg for mercy and plead with him for her people. She sent word back reminding him of the law that stated that if anyone approached the king in the inner court without being summoned they would be put to death. The only exception was if the king were to extend his golden scepter to them and spare their life. And, Esther informed Mordecai that the king had not sent for her in a full month. Mordecai sent her back a very powerful reply, saying:

> *"Don't think that just because you are the Queen that you will not face destruction, too. And if you remain silent at this time, relief and deliverance for the Jews will arise from another place, but you and your family will perish. And who knows, perhaps you have come to royal position for such a time as this."* (Esther 4:13b, 14)

Scene 9: For such a time as this!

Well, that did it for Esther. She realized that this could be the greatest purpose of her life. She sent back her reply saying for Mordecai to gather all of the Jews in the area and that they along with Esther and her maids should fast and pray for three days. Then, she said, *"When this fast is over, I will go to the king, even though it is against the law. And if I perish, I perish"* (Esther 4:16).

When the three days were over, Esther put on her royal robes and went to the inner court of the king. He was pleased to see her and extended the golden scepter to her. Then he asked, *"Queen Esther, what is your request? Whatever it is, it will be given to you, even up to half the kingdom"* (Esther 5:3). Esther wisely waited for the right time to discuss her people's plight, and instead invited the king and Haman to a banquet that she had prepared for them. They immediately went to the banquet where the king again asked Esther concerning her request. She responded that she requested that he and Haman return tomorrow for another banquet, at which time she would answer his question.

Haman went home that night very puffed up about being invited to the queen's banquets. On his way home, he saw Mordecai who neither bowed, nor showed fear in his presence. This infuriated Haman. He went home and gathered all of his friends and family, bragging to them about being invited to Queen Esther's banquets. But, he confessed that this satisfaction was diminished every time he saw Mordecai. His wife and friends suggested that he have gallows built, seventy-five feet high, and ask the king in the morning to have Mordecai hanged on it. This suggestion delighted Haman and he had the gallows built.

Scene 10: As good as Ambien.

That night, the king could not sleep so he ordered that the book of the annals be brought in and read to him. It had been recorded there that Mordecai had exposed the assassination plan of the king, thus saving his life. The king realized that nothing had ever been done to show his appreciation to Mordecai. Right at that time, Haman came to the outer court to ask the king to give permission to hang Mordecai. The king called Haman in, but before he could ask the king asked him what should be done for someone who pleased the king. Thinking proudly that the king was referring to himself, Haman replied that that man should receive one of the king's royal robes and royal crests and royal horses and be led throughout the city, proclaiming before him, *"This is what is done for the man the king delights to honor"* (Esther 6:6). The king then commanded Haman to go at once and do for Mordecai just as he had suggested. So Haman had to lead Mordecai through the streets, announcing that the king delighted in him. He was mortified, of course, but soon after had to go to Queen Esther's banquet.

Scene 11: *Vengeance is mine, says the Lord!*

At the banquet, the king once again asked Queen Esther what her request was, and vowed that whatever it was it would be granted, up to half the kingdom. At that time, Esther revealed her request: that he would grant her life, and also spare the lives of her people. Not knowing that she was of Jewish descent, the king did not know what she was talking about. He asked, *"Who is he? Who would dare to do such a thing?"* (Esther 7:5). She replied, *"The adversary and enemy is this vile Haman"* (Esther 7:6). The king was enraged, and Haman was terrified. The king

"It's not about you. The purpose of your life is far greater than your own personal fulfillment, your peace of mind, or even your happiness. It's far greater than your family, your career, or even your wildest dreams and ambitions. If you want to know why you were placed on this planet, you must begin with God. You were born by his purpose and or his purpose. The search for the purpose of life has puzzled people for thousands of years. That's because we typically begin at the wrong starting point—ourselves. We ask self-centered questions like What do I want to be? What should I do with my life? What are my goals, my ambitions, my dreams for my future? But focusing on our selves will never reveal our life's purpose... You were made by God and for God—and until you understand that, life will never make sense."viii

Stephen Grellet (1773-1855) wrote,

"I expect to pass through life but once. If, therefore, there be any kind ness I can show, or any good thing I can do to any fellow being, let me do it now. Let me not defer nor neglect it, for I shall not pass this way again."ix

I believe that we should look at each day of our life as a divine opportunity to once again die to self, take up the cross and follow Him. You never know when you may come to that "for such a time as this" moment. Will you be ready? You don't have to be a queen or king, or even have a degree from a reputable seminary. You don't have to try to be something that you are not. You simply have to trust, like Esther did, that your ordinary life is in the hands of an extraordinary God!

Ordinary Used for the Extraordinary

As I have said before, while living in Costa Rica we taught a Bible School each Saturday in an area called Los Guidos. Each week, we brought God's truth to the poor children who lived in shacks along a mountainside. The streets were dirt, and there were only specific times that the public buses would make their rounds through that area. The neighborhood was full of crime and we were told not to be there after dark. One day, after a fun, full time of leading Bible schools for the children, we were waiting for the bus to take us back to the San Jose area where we were living. The bus was late, so we passed the time by talking to the children gathered near the bus stop.

I began to talk to a little girl who was about eight years old. I asked her in Spanish if she knew Jesus. She just stared at me with a look of confusion. Thinking that perhaps she misunderstood my pronunciation, I reworded the question. Her face still showed confusion and lack of understanding, and she slowly shook her head and said, "No". I realized that not only did she not know the Lord as Savior, but she had never even heard of Him. About that time we heard the bus making its slow progress down the hill. It was the last bus of the day and we could not miss it.

I began to quickly pray for wisdom, and out of the corner of my eye I saw another little eight-year-old girl that I knew. She faithfully came to our weekly Bible Schools, and I knew that she had a knowledge and love for Jesus. I pulled her aside and quickly asked her if she knew Jesus. She said yes, and then I said, "What do you know about Jesus?"

The sounds of the approaching bus began to get louder and

louder, as I nervously listened to my little friend stating all that she knew about Jesus: He was God's own son, He died on the cross to save us from our sins, He rose again on the third day, He healed people, He took the little boy's lunch and fed all the people around Him. Just as the bus approached our bus stop, I led my friend to the lost little girl and said, "Tell her everything that you know to be true about Jesus." I then turned and ran to the bus just before it pulled away from the bus stop.

As I sat in my seat looking out the window, I saw my friend—my little sister in Christ—speaking to the lost girl with diligence and animation. And the lost girl was listening intently to what she said. As we drove away from Los Guidos, I was struck by that picture: two little girls, in a sea of poverty, having a conversation that could make an eternal difference in the lives of so many—in that little girl's life as well as her family, her friends, and the generation to come through her. And all I could do was pray. I was humbled by the fact that it was not about me, anyway. Only the Holy Spirit can convict someone and draw him or her unto the throne of God. And really, anyone can be used as a vessel for the Father to accomplish His great and mighty purposes, even an eight-year-old girl who knew basic truth.

Ten years later, I observed a similar situation to that Costa Rican experience. We had moved from Tupelo, Mississippi to nearby Corinth, Mississippi. It was spring break and our dear friends, the Bean family, had driven from Tupelo to Corinth to spend the day with us. The Beans had lived across the street from us in Tupelo and we were all very close friends. We shared a love for Christ, a membership at the same church, and we looked to each other for support and prayer and friendship. A beautiful friendship had developed between my daughter, Ellie, and the Bean's daughter, Lauren. Ellie had recently asked Jesus to be her Lord and Savior, and was very disturbed to find out that Lauren had not yet taken that step. I assured her that she had nothing to worry about—Lauren knew of Jesus, and loved Him, and I was confident that she indeed would be a follower of Christ. Ellie walked away from our conversation with a concerned and thoughtful look on her face.

The two moms went off to shop while a sitter kept the children at our house to play. When we returned, our girls were giggling and laughing and looking at each other, as if they had a delightful secret between them. Lauren asked her mom to go into another room with her so that she could tell her the reason for their joy—Ellie had prayed with Lauren to receive Christ! Ellie explained to me that she continued to feel burdened for Lauren, and while we were gone, she began to tell Lauren all she knew to be true about Jesus, and about her eight-year-old experiences of following Him.

About a month later, Lauren came before the church to be baptized. They shared their story, through video, with the congregation, and our Pastor, Bryan Collier, asked Ellie to come stand with him as he baptized Lauren as a symbol of her being resurrected into a new life in Christ. Two little girls, having a conversation that will make an eternal difference in the lives of so many—in both girls' lives, as well as their families, their friends, and the generations to come through them. And, once again, I was humbled by the fact that it was not about me, anyway.

The Four P's

What we learn from the story of Esther can be summed up in the following way:

Preparation

Perspective

Prayer

Praise

Preparation: God wants to prepare us for the extraordinary. We can only receive that preparation by reaching up to Him. That is why I have repeatedly emphasized the concept of Reaching Up to God. You prepare for the extraordinary by letting God be God in your life. He wants to be your redeemer. He wants to use even the difficult circumstances in your life to show His mighty power and His glory. He will also use His Word, godly people, and His Holy Spirit to prepare you for the extraordinary.

Perspective: We should seek God's perspective in every situation, knowing that we will never be able to—this side of heaven—see the whole tapestry of our lives. Esther could not have known all the many ways her story of obedience and purpose would bear fruit even thousands of years later. To have a godly perspective our eyes must be on Him, not on us. It is about trusting that He is able to do far more than we could ever hope, or dream, or imagine, even if we don't see the end of the story.

Prayer: I don't exactly know how prayer works, but it does.

Sometimes prayer changes situations, but always prayer changes me. Prayer is honest communication with God. Prayer is talking and listening. Prayer is acknowledging God's power and acknowledging your weakness. Esther fasted and prayed for three days (there's that holy three again!) before she went before the king. And she got others to pray with her and for her. Prayer is crucial in finding and participating in God's extraordinary plan for your life. Ephesians 2:10 says, *"For you are God's workmanship, created in Christ Jesus to do good works, which God prepared in advance for us to do."* Pray that God will show you the good works that He has prepared for you!

Praise: Lastly, the outcome of the extraordinary purpose and plan for Esther resulted in praise to God alone. Recently I read a book by Steve Saint where he described being in Israel during the Feast of Purim. Through that feast, centuries after the fact, there is still much praise and celebration toward our extraordinary God for the extraordinary work He did in and through Esther, an ordinary girl. Our ordinary ways, surrendered to His will can produce extraordinary fruit. God loves to use the ordinary to produce the extraordinary. Because when extraordinary things happen in and through the ordinary, the glory and honor and praise go to Him alone.

Chapter 11
What's In a Name?

One Christmas, my mother took great care to prepare a very special gift for her 10 grandchildren: She researched the biblical meaning behind each of their names, complete with a corresponding scripture, and had a calligrapher create a beautifully framed inscription of the results. Though it was not the most expensive or elaborate gift that they received that year, it was definitely the most meaningful—to the giver, as well as the recipient. The following was the result of my mother's research:

Katie—Godly Example. *"So that you will prove yourselves to be blameless and innocent, children of God above reproach..."*

(Phil. 2:15; NAS)

Ellie—Shining Light. *"If you are filled with light, with no dark corners, then your whole life will be radiant, as though a floodlight were filling you with light."* (Luke 11:36)

Joseph—Wise and Understanding. *"Those who seek the Lord understand all."* (Prov. 28:5; NKJ)

Troy—Steadfast. *"God is able to make all grace abound to you, so that always having all sufficiency in everything, you may have an abundance for every good deed."* (2 Cor.9:8; NAS)

Joshua—Truth Seeker. *"But he who looks into the perfect law of liberty and continues in it—this one will be blessed in what he does."* (James 1:25; NKJ)

As a mother, I was amazed at how accurately the meanings depicted the personalities and attributes of my children. Each child seems to exhibit what their name represents. For example, my "Truth Seeker," Joshua is a very literal young boy. Things in his mind are true or false, right or wrong. One day, when Joshua was about two-and-a-half years old, I called to my daughter, Ellie, to ask her to bring something to me. In doing so, I said, "Angel, will you bring me…." Joshua stopped what he was doing, looked up at me and said, "Why you call her 'angel'? She not 'angel', she Ellie!"

When we named each of our children, we prayerfully considered what their names would imply. Some names were eliminated simply by the fact that other people with the same name acted in ways that we did not want our children to follow. All of the names were picked because of others that held the same name had proved to be great followers of God.

We picked the name Joshua, because of Joshua, son of Nun, found in the Scriptures. We felt that our Joshua would also be called of God to be "strong and courageous," especially being the fifth rung on the family ladder! And we wanted him to also realize that God would always be with him no matter what. Further study of Scripture reveals more meanings of the name

Joshua. In Zechariah 3, we find a vision concerning the high priest, Joshua, son of Jehozadak. We find that this same name was spelled "Jeshua" in other scriptural references x (Ezra 2:2 and Nehemiah 7:7) Both names were from the same root and were very common names in ancient times. In fact, the Greek equivalent is spelled "Jesus" in English. What a beautiful picture of our Lord and Savior, the King of Kings selected to be named and reared as a common man; fully God, yet fully man— ordinary earthly beginnings, yet never diminishing, extraordinary perfect deity.

All three of these names, Joshua, Jeshua and Jesus have the further meaning, "The Lord saves". Of course, only the Lord Jesus of Nazareth has the definitive completion of the meaning; all other Joshuas are the recipients of the meaning. Jesus, born of ordinary, extraordinarily saves all the ordinary "Joshuas" that turn to Him. So I present to you the thought, as we continue to study Joshua, son of Nun, as well as Joshua, son of Jehozadak, that another symbolic meaning for use in our present study is Joshua the ordinary man. Once again, we will see how God loves to use the ordinary for His extraordinary purposes.

Read the following vision, given to Zechariah, a beautiful, symbolic picture of our place before the judgment throne:

> *"Then the Lord showed me Joshua the high priest standing before the angel of the Lord, and Satan standing at his right side to accuse him. The Lord said to Satan, 'The Lord rebuke you, Satan! The Lord, who has chosen Jerusalem, rebuke you! Is not this man a burning stick snatched from the fire?'*

"Now Joshua was dressed in filthy clothes as he stood before the angel. The angel said to those who were standing before him, 'Take off his filthy clothes.' Then he said to Joshua, 'See, I have taken away your sin, and I will put rich garments on you.' Then I said, 'Put a clean turban on his head.' So they put a clean turban on his head, and clothed him, while the angel of the Lord stood by.

"The angel of the Lord gave this charge to Joshua: 'This is what the Lord Almighty says: 'If you walk in my ways and keep my require-ments, then you will govern my house and have charge of my courts, and I will give you a place among these standing here. 'Listen, O high priest Joshua and your associates seated before you, who are men sym-bolic of things to come: I am going to bring my servant, the Branch. See, the stone I have set in front of Joshua! There are seven eyes on that one stone, and I will engrave an inscription on it,' says the Lord Al-mighty, 'and I will remove the sin of this land in a single day. 'In that day each of you will invite his neighbor to sit under his vine and fig tree, declares the Lord Almighty.'"

(Zechariah 3:1-10)

This vision was given to Zechariah about his friend Joshua. Just after this vision, another was given to describe to Zechariah the anointing that was about to come to Joshua and Zerubbabel so that they could serve the Lord in an extraordinary way. And all the power would come from God, not from their own feeble efforts, for God gave this word: *"Not by might nor by power, but by my Spirit', says the Lord Almighty"* (Zech. 4:6). But the initial vision had to be fulfilled first. Work needed to be done to prepare the ordinary for the extraordinary. Picture the vision as if it courtroom scene: Joshua standing before the angel of th.. with Satan right beside him continually accusing him. Were the accusations accurate? Perhaps, but that is not the point. The point is that the Lord stepped in to defend. The Lord Himself rebuked Satan, declaring that Joshua was a burning stick snatched from the fire.

What a beautiful description. Joshua, ordinary man, was snatched by God himself from the eternal destruction of a fiery hell. That is me, too. God snatched me from the fire when He graciously saved me. And to further bless my soul (and yours, if you are a believer), He declares in John 10:27-29 that, *"My sheep listen to my voice; I know them, and they follow me. I give them eternal life, and they shall never perish; no one can snatch them out of my hand. My Father, who has given them to me, is greater than all; no one can snatch them out of my Father's hand."* What a beautiful picture! The Father will not let go of His people. He will personally defend them, snatch them from the fire, and not let go!

Next, we see that as the accuser is forced to leave the scene, the repair work begins. Joshua was standing there in filthy clothes. Those clothes represented the priestly order, and taking them off represented removal from the priestly office. Yet, this was also representative of the removal of sin. Perhaps Joshua was in all appearances a "priest," yet God saw his heart. In the same way, we often have an effective Christ-like appearance on the outside—we go to church, tithe, talk the talk, etc., but what about the state of our hearts. I, too, have had times that God exposed my "filthy clothes," only to reveal a heart that was in desperate need of revival.

u? Is God calling you to the humbling posi-
ng, even if only to yourself, that you too need
ur filthy clothes removed? If so, there is good news
ne! Listen to what God says directly to Joshua just after
e filth had been exposed: *"See, I have taken away your sin, and I will put rich garments on you"* (Zech. 3:4). What grace and mercy is displayed in those words. Mercy is not getting the punishment and death that we deserve. We could never get rid of our filthy clothes on our own merit. Only God can take away our sins.

But then He goes even further. He does not leave us un-clothed, in shame and embarrassment. He then promises to clothe us with rich garments! In fact, Romans 13:14 says *"Clothe yourselves with the Lord Jesus Christ."* No brand of clothing could ever compare to these rich garments! That is the grace of God in action. Grace is getting what we don't deserve. It is receiving far more than we could ever hope, or dream, or imagine (Ephe-sians 3:20). God takes the ordinary man, removes the sin and obstacles that hold him back, then clothes him in preparation for the extraordinary work that God has planned for him.

As we see in the vision, a clean turban is put on his head. This action re-instated him into the high-priestly order, only now with the purity and holiness and power that could not come from ordinary man, but only from the Holy Spirit. Now he is ready for the extraordinary work. But the experience was not complete without the acceptance of the charge laid before Joshua:

> *"This is what the Lord Almighty says: 'If you will walk in my ways and keep my requirements, then you will govern my house and have*

charge of my courts, and I will give you a place among these standing here. Listen, O high priest Joshua and your associates seated before you, who are men symbolic of things to come: I am going to bring my servant, the Branch. See, the stone I have set in front of Joshua! There are seven eyes on that one stone, and I will engrave an inscription on it,' says the Lord Almighty, 'and I will remove the sin of this land in a single day. In that day each of you will invite his neighbor to sit under his vine and fig tree, declares the Lord Almighty." (Zech. 3:7-10)

This charge sounds much like the charge laid before Joshua, son of Nun in Joshua 1:7-8:

"Be strong and very courageous. Be careful to obey all the law my servant Moses gave you; do not turn from it to the right or to the left, that you may be successful wherever you go. Do not let this Book of the Law depart from your mouth; meditate on it day and night, so that you may be careful to do everything written in it. Then you will be prosperous and successful."

You see there is a cause and effect in action. There is a charge that we have to keep. Though it clearly is not based on our own good actions, there is an acceptance of the charge. There is a "if you, then I" principal. God clearly says, "If you follow in my ways, then I will anoint you for extraordinary success." And as if that promise was not thrilling enough, God added something even more phenomenal! God did not want the significance to be lost, so He prefaced it with the word, "Listen". When I am telling something important to my children and I want them to understand the importance of what I am saying, I will often use that preface of "Now, Listen!" In the same way, God wanted Joshua and his associates to understand the importance of what was to come: *"Listen…I am going to bring my servant, the Branch"* (Zech. 3:7, 8). That is a Messianic title. He was talking about Jesus. Note the comparison of Joshua, ordinary man, as a burning stick, and Jesus, the Branch, with a capital B! We are nothing, He is everything! Yet, He was sent for us!

God again prefaces His announcement with an attention grabber word, "See". It is as if He is saying, "Don't you see the significance!" There is a stone set before ordinary man, Joshua; a stone with seven eyes, perhaps symbolic of the completion and perfection of the stone. And this same stone is engraved with an inscription and a promise for the instant removal of sin. This sounds very much like what we find in Isaiah 49:15, 16: *"Can a mother forget the baby at her breast and have no compassion on the child she has borne? Though she may forget, I will not forget you! See, I have engraved you on the palms of my hands…"*

We find in Exodus 28:9-12 that the names of the tribes of Israel were engraved on stones and fastened to the ephod of the high priest as a memorial before the Lord. At the cross, Jesus, the greatest high priest, the Chief Cornerstone, engraved our names on His palms as a memorial and remembrance before the Lord. He will not forget you if you are His! No matter what happens, God will not forget His children. The removal of sin in a single day refers to the day that Christ died for us. And what should our reaction be to all of this? *"In that day each of you will invite his neighbor to sit under his vine and fig tree, declares the Lord Almighty"* (Zech. 3:10).

After I began studying these scriptures, I came across the

"vine and fig tree" phrase many places in the Bible. When the truths finally hit home, our reaction should be two-fold: first, "sit under his vine and fig tree," according to the NIV study Bible, is a "proverbial picture of peace, security, and contentment." xi And secondly, we should invite our neighbors to join us! How are we doing in these two areas? Have we forgotten what has been done for us? Do we really "get it"? If we stop and think, and remember, then we will be a "proverbial picture of peace, security and contentment," and that alone should be such a witness to our "neighbors," or anyone that we come into contact with, that they, too, will want to come and receive what we have so graciously been given.

The Name

Several years ago, my niece Elizabeth went to see the Easter program at the First Evangelical Church in Tupelo, Mississippi. For years they put on an incredibly anointed drama of the story of Jesus. One climactic part is a scene in which Jesus, sitting on His throne of glory is holding a large book. As He sees the joyful ones entering into the glorious heavenly realm, He marks off their name in the book. That night, when my brother was putting Elizabeth to bed, she asked, "Daddy, what was that big book that Jesus was holding at the end of the play?" "Why, honey that was the Book of Life. Jesus writes the name of all of His followers, everyone who knows Him and is going to heaven, in the Book of Life." Elizabeth thought for a moment, and then looked up at her dad and said, "I want my name in that book, Daddy." And they both kneeled down beside her bed and took care of it then and there.

me? What's in my name? What do people
en they hear my name? Do they think of ma-
Jo they think of social activities? Do they think
auty? Do they think of accomplishments? None
of   ngs are wrong, but is that the main thing that they
think?

Do they think of love or arrogance? Do they think of truth
or lies? Do they think of sincerity or just southern manners?
Do they think of humility or pride? Do they think of service or
self-centeredness? Do they think of grace or bitterness?

And the most important question of all: When they hear my
name, do they think of The Name? The Name that is above
all names, the King of all kings, the Lord of all lords, the Alpha
and the Omega, the Beginning and the End, the Redeemer, the
Mighty God, the Wonderful Counselor, the Prince of Peace, the
Lamb of God, the Great Physician, the Great Shepherd—all
of these names are synonymous with one beautiful name, the
Name of Jesus.

According to Philippians 2:9-11:

> *"Therefore God exalted him to the highest place and gave him the name
> that is above every name, that at the name of Jesus every knee should
> bow, in heaven and on earth and under the earth, and every tongue
> confess that Jesus Christ is Lord, to the glory of God the Father."*

I don't know about you, but my heart longs to be associated
with that perfect Name! I pray that when someone hears my
name, they will think of The Name. Yet that is a great respon-

sibility. Because once we associate with The Name, then we are a reflection of the Name. Are we an accurate reflection of that wonderful Name?

Throughout biblical history we find repeatedly that there is emphasis made on someone's name. In *The Prayer of Jabez* by Bruce H. Wilkinson there is great emphasis on the fact that Jabez meant "sorrow maker". The prayer that Jabez prayed was a prayer to overcome the meaning of the name and all the implications that followed the name. Proverbs 22:1 tells us that *"A good name is more desirable than great riches."* For many reasons that I don't fully understand, a person's name is valuable and can help or hinder someone.

Before we take this too literally, I need to explain that most of the value or hindrance attached to a name is in the spiritual realm. There are many examples in the Bible in which God changes a particular person's name so that they can rise above life's circumstances and fulfill all that God's plan intends for them to fulfill. A few common examples are the following:

- **Abraham:** Abram to Abraham. Abram meant "exalted father". This is ironic because his greatest struggle was the infertility that he and Sarah experienced. Abraham meant "Father of Many". God was preparing him for the extraordinary. Not only would he become a father, but would become the father that had as many descendents as the sands of the ocean.

- **Sarah:** Sarah was first Sarai. Both names meant "princess," but Sarah meant "God's princess"—preparing the ordinary for the extraordinary

- **Jacob:** Jacob meant "deceiver". After persistent wrestling with spiritual issues, God changed his name to Israel, which meant "Prince of God". The deceiver became a nobleman, royalty in God's Kingdom.

- **Paul:** Saul the persecutor became Paul the apostle.
- **Peter:** Simon became Peter, the rock on which God built His church, and this was after he betrayed the very One who was going to do the extraordinary work.
- **Joshua:** Even Joshua had a name change. His original name was Hosea, which meant salvation. Joshua means, "The Lord saves". Moses, through prompting and a prophetic word from God, gave Joshua this new name right before he went into the Promised Land the first time as one of the 12 spies. The meaning of his new name bore fruit, first at this time when he returned and he and Caleb were the only ones to believe that God could save. They stood up and said, "*...do not be afraid of the people of the land, because we will swallow them up. Their protection is gone, but the Lord is with us*" (Num. 14:9). He trusted in the Lord's salvation, not his own! And that trust continued throughout his lifetime.

In each of those examples we see a two-part process. First, there was relationship with God, and then there was significant change in their ordinary lives which prepared them for the extraordinary. We don't need to change our names to be used of God. The point is not really about the names themselves. The point is about us and our view of us. How do you view yourself? There are two opposite extremes that are equally dangerous and wrong. One extreme is the puffed up, prideful person who thinks very highly of himself. Let's look at what the Word has to say about that type of person:

"For by the grace given me I say to every one of you: Do
yourself more highly than you ought, but rather think of
self with sober judgment, in accordance with the measure of
faith God has given you."

(Romans 12:3)

"Pride goes before destruction, a haughty spirit before a fall."
(Proverbs 16:18)

What I find more often among women is the opposite extreme. So many women are bound by the negative view that they have of themselves. Self-image and self-esteem are hot topics these days because so many people are crippled by a misplaced view of themselves. I say misplaced because our tendency is to view ourselves through the eyes of the world, through what others think about us, or maybe even through our past. Many times our past cripples our ability to be fruitful and fulfilled in our present and our future. And that is just what the enemy of our soul wants to happen.

But God has a different plan for us. He wants us to view ourselves in the way that He sees us. Yes, He knows our sin. Yes, He knows our past. Yes, He knows everything about us. But this is an example of how He views us:

"The LORD your God is with you, he is mighty to save. He will take
great delight in you, he will quiet you with his love, he will rejoice over
you with singing." (Zephaniah 3:17)

"The LORD appeared to us in the past, saying: 'I have loved you with an everlasting love; I have drawn you with loving-kindness…" (Jeremiah 31:3)

"He who has an ear, let him hear what the Spirit says to the churches. To him who overcomes, I will give some of the hidden manna. I will also give him a white stone with a new name written on it, known only to him who receives it." (Revelation 2:17)

In heaven, we, the children of God will be given a precious white stone with a new name inscribed on it. This holy 'nickname' will be just between us and God; a holy, loving symbolism of all He sees in us through His never-failing eyes of love.

Chapter 12
A Fruitful Future

In Genesis we find a small but very significant account pertaining to our topic of what is in a name. I'm sure you remember Joseph and his coat of many colors. Do you remember his painful past? He was a favorite of his father, but hated by his brothers. His brothers sold him into slavery and he was put in jail for a crime he didn't commit. His troubles were numerous. But he had God's favor, and eventually he had the favor of Pharaoh.

Joseph is famous for forgiving his brothers many years later when he found himself in a royal position over them. He could have been bitter and gotten revenge. But instead he said, *"What you meant for evil, God meant for good"* (Gen. 50:20). Eventually, because of a severe famine, his entire family came to live under his care in Egypt. It was in Egypt that his father, Jacob, now renamed Israel, found himself at the time of his death. We find in Genesis 41:50 that Joseph had two sons:

*"Before the years of famine came, two sons were born to Joseph...
Joseph named his firstborn Manasseh and said, 'It is because God has
made me forget all my trouble and all my father's household.' The
second son he named Ephraim and said, 'It is because God has made
me fruitful in the land of my suffering."*

(Genesis 41:50-52)

The names of Joseph's sons are positive in an odd kind of
way: Manasseh's name is indicative of his painful past while
Ephraim's name is indicative of his fruitful future.

This is what happened. When Jacob/Israel was on his death
bed, he called all of his sons together so that he could pass on
the blessing. This was very important in that culture as it was
not just about monetary or material blessing, but it was emotion-
al and spiritual blessing. They literally needed the blessing from
the father to be successful in their future. A lack of blessing
would be crippling.

Though we don't necessarily hold to the same tradition, the
principles are still true for us today. How many people are emotionally crippled because they never received a "blessing," physical touch and kind, positive, affirming words, from their parents,
especially their father? I know countless numbers of people that
can pinpoint the problems of their past and present to this issue.

It has become popular to blame our parents for every sin or
hang-up that we encounter or fall prey to. This should not be.
Our parents are not to blame for all of our problems. Though
there are tragic episodes of abuse or neglect, even then forgiveness must come, lest the victim remain a crippled victim

for a lifetime. Sometimes healing must take place in our lives. No human father, or mother, can fulfill our needs or heal our hurts. We will hurt our kids at times. But we must point them constantly to the perfect father, God, who can meet their every need. And we must look constantly to Him to meet our every need.

If our parents, or anyone for that matter, have hurt us, we must free them from our lack of forgiveness so that we do not put ourselves into bondage. Unforgiveness quickly binds us up emotionally and spiritually and opens a wide door for Satan to wreak havoc in our lives. We can never be more like Jesus than when we have to forgive.

Joseph was deeply hurt by his family, yet he forgave. And he was blessed by God. As a result of his pain, his father wanted to give him a double portion of inheritance and blessing. To do that, Jacob claimed Manasseh and Ephraim as his own sons, not his grandsons, and he instructed Joseph to bring in both sons to receive the blessing. This is what happened…

"And Joseph took both of them, Ephraim on his right toward Israel's left hand and Manasseh on his left toward Israel's right hand, and brought them close to him. But Israel reached out his right hand and put it on Ephraim's head, though he was the younger, and crossing his arms, he put his left hand on Manasseh's head, even though Manasseh was the firstborn.

"Then he blessed Joseph and said,

> *'May the God before whom my fathers*
> *Abraham and Isaac walked,*
> *the God who has been my shepherd*

all my life to this day,
"the Angel who has delivered me from all harm
—may he bless these boys.
May they be called by my name
and the names of my fathers Abraham and Isaac,
and may they increase greatly
upon the earth.'
"When Joseph saw his father placing his right hand on Ephraim's
head he was displeased; so he took hold of his father's hand to move
it from Ephraim's head to Manasseh's head. Joseph said to him, 'No,
my father, this one is the firstborn; put your right hand on his head.'
"But his father refused and said, 'I know, my son, I know. He too will
become a people, and he too will become great. Nevertheless, his younger
brother will be greater than he, and his descendants will become a group
of nations.' He blessed them that day and said,
'In your name will Israel pronounce this blessing:
'May God make you like Ephraim and Manasseh.'
So he put Ephraim ahead of Manasseh." (Genesis 48:13-20)

When I first read that passage I was really intrigued by it. I never studied it in Sunday school, nor heard a sermon on it. It bugged me because I didn't really get it. One night I woke Mont up and tried to tell him all about it, but he was too sleepy. The next morning, Mont said, "What in the world were you talking about...crossing arms?!" So I kept studying it. One day, I was looking for something to read and I came across a book on my shelf that I didn't remember buying, and have no idea where it came from. It was called *The Forgotten Blessing* by Aaron Fruh, a Jewish Christian. It had powerful insight into this very passage.

Remember, the meaning of Manasseh's name was indicative of a very painful past. The name Ephraim, the second born, was indicative of a fruitful future. When Jacob crossed his arms he was making a bold statement, saying from this day forward the fruitfulness of the future would take precedence over the pain of the past. In many people's lives the opposite is true—the past hinders the fruitfulness of their life. And that is exactly what the enemy of your soul wants for you. If Satan can keep you caught up in the pain or shame of your past, he can hinder how fruitful and abundant your life is. Don't let that happen! You can find all the healing you need by totally surrendering to the Great Physician, Jesus. And the reason that I know this is because of one more powerful and prophetic truth found in this passage.

I say prophetic because it is another mirror image of something that would take place many generations later. At the cross, God, our perfect parent, crossed his arms for us! For one powerful moment in time God put his right hand of blessing on us, and let His first born Son, Jesus, carry the weight of every painful past. The scripture says, *"By his stripes, we are healed"* (Isa. 53:5; NKJ). It is because of this "crossing of His arms," and because Jesus was willing to be placed in that position that the fruitfulness of our present and future can take precedence over any pain of our past. We can be totally free! And that is very good news!

The Names of God

We cannot end this chapter without spending a moment reflecting on The Name, and all the many implications and power of this precious Name. In Scripture, we find that God has many descriptive aspects of His Name. Think for a minute on the following sampling of the mighty Names of our Lord. Pray that the truth of these Names and what they mean to you and me will penetrate the rough and wounded places of our souls.

Elohim—God
Jehovah/Yahweh—The self-existent one: I Am
Jehovah-Jireh—The Lord will provide
Jehovah-Rapha—The Lord who heals
Jehovah-Nissi—The Lord is our banner
Jehovah-Shalom—The Lord is our peace
Jehovah-Ra-ah—The Lord is my shepherd
Jehovah-Tsidkenu—The Lord is our righteousness
Jehovah-Shammah—The Lord is present
Jehovah-Elohim—The Lord God
Jehovah-Sabaoth—The Lord of Hosts
El Elyon—The Most High God
Adonai—Our Master
El Shaddai—Almighty God, The Strength Giver
El Olam—Everlasting God

Jesus said, "I am…"
- The Resurrection
- The Way
- The Truth
- The Life
- The Light of the World
- The Bread of Life

- The Good Shepherd
- The Door of the Sheep
- The True Vine
- The Great Physician
- Wonderful
- Counselor
- Mighty God
- Prince of Peace

"The stone the builders rejected has become the capstone; the Lord has done this, and it is marvelous in our eyes. This is the day the Lord has made; let us rejoice and be glad in it." (Psalm 118:22-24)

He is the Stone of Remembrance! With this Stone of Remembrance on our side, we can boldly reach up to God, reach out to others, and remember that He is an extraordinary God who chooses to do extraordinary things in ordinary people.

The
Stone
of
Worship

Chapter 13
Preparation for the
Extraordinary

We began our study with Joshua. And we have learned that like Joshua, there are three important overall lessons that we must learn: Reach Up, Reach Out, and Remember. Now I want to touch on the question of how Joshua got to the place where he could be used by an extraordinary God for an extraordinary purpose. To understand this we can't just start at the spot where his leadership began; we have to start with his time of preparation for leadership when he was mentored under Moses, and even further back to Moses' parents.

We don't hear a lot of information about Moses' parents, but we know that their faith and courage was passed on to Moses, who passed it on to Joshua, and this serves as an example for us all. The beauty of the plan is that one legacy of faith is passed to another. One life touches another, who touches another, and another, and another. Together, not separately, this forms an extraordinary tapestry of God's plan; all using ordinary people who believe in an extraordinary God. It excites and amazes me to think of it! And, if you have a relationship with Jesus Christ, then you can count on the fact that you are a part of the tapestry.

Joshua grew up as a slave in Egypt. He knew first-hand the hardships of slavery. And then came Moses! When we think of Moses, we think of a chosen one; the great and mighty. When we think of Moses, we think of an anointed one of God, used as a mighty instrument—a small foreshadowing of what was to come through Jesus, the One who frees all men from the eternal slavery of sin and death. But Moses was used of God in spite of himself.

Let's look at who Moses was leading up to his mighty days:
- He did have a special anointing, even as a child. Hebrews 11 tells us that his parents saw that he was a special child, yet, he was still born a slave with a death sentence on his tiny head. It would be literally impossible for greatness to occur in his life. Yet, as Jesus told us in Mark 10:27, *"With man this is impossible, but with God, all things are possible."*
- As an act of faith by his parents, Moses was delivered from a sure death sentence. The vehicle of deliverance was an ordinary basket used by slaves for ordinary tasks. God can and will use the ordinary to deliver the extraordinary!
- As the Lord intended, this ordinary basket caught the eye of royalty. The princess ordered that the basket be snatched from the river, and a slave child was discovered. What was the princess thinking to want to save a slave child, especially in light of all of the killings that were going on at the time—killings ordered by her own family! Do you

not see a parallel of the prompting that resulted in the action? It was God who prompted her to retrieve that slave basket, because God, too, saw more than just an ordinary slave basket. God saw inside the basket. God saw more than a slave child. God saw His anointed, chosen one.

No matter what ordinary wrappings you have, God sees you as a chosen one. *"You did not choose me, I chose you and appointed you to go and bear fruit—fruit that will last"* (John 15:16). He chose you for a special appointment, just as he chose Moses for his special appointment. Will you accept the appointment and, as my pastor often says,"choose your chosen-ness"? And then God says to go and bear fruit: the fruit of the Spirit—love, joy, peace, patience, kindness, goodness, gentleness, faithfulness and self-control. And only with the power and anointing of the Holy Spirit will it be healthy fruit that will last.

Yes, people can do good things that help our society. Humanitarian and social efforts can produce good changes. But true, lasting fruit can only be produced when someone starts to realize and act like a chosen one who has accepted an appointment. With that first step, with that surrender of our own will and feeble efforts, God is pleased. And when God is pleased, great things begin to happen! We step aside, and He steps in. He uses our ordinary status and brings about His extraordinary work.

The word 'Go' obviously involves action on our part. And it is not a suggestion, such as, "if you feel led, go" or "if you aren't too busy, go". It is a direct command for every believer: "Go!" We find it again in the most powerful commission of all:

"Then the eleven disciples went to Galilee, to the mountain where Jesus had told them to go. When they saw him, they worshiped him; but some doubted. Then Jesus came to them and said, 'All authority in heaven and on earth has been given to me. Therefore go and make disciples of all nations, baptizing them in the name of the Father and of the Son and of the Holy Spirit, and teaching them to obey every thing I have commanded you. And surely I am with you always, to the very end of the age.'" (Matthew 28:17-20)

If you knew that you were about to go to heaven in the next few minutes, what would you say to your family and close friends? Would you not think through and carefully word your last statements so that they would be remembered and cherished. Would you not take that opportunity to say things that are of extreme importance, not just casual conversation? Of course you would want to carefully speak, if you knew you were heaven bound! And so it was with Jesus.

Matthew 28:18-20 is known as The Great Commission, and it was the last instructions that Jesus gave His followers before He ascended into heaven. It was very important, and it was meant for all of the family of God, every believer then and now and in the future. And the command was to "Go!" Now it is not my place to tell you where to go; God will readily tell you that, if you are courageous enough to ask Him. But as a fellow believer, I can remind you that we all must "Go", and as we go, we must make disciples. We all must reach out to others. We all are God's workmanship, and all have good works that He wants us to do, which He has prepared in advance for us.

Worship is part of the preparation for the extraordinary plan God has for your life. Notice, in the Matthew 28 passage, that the disciples obeyed and went where Jesus told them to go. They would have missed it if they had not listened and obeyed. Next, we see that they saw Jesus. We must open our eyes to see Him. We must seek Him, daily. We must learn enough about Him that we recognize Him and His Voice in our lives. When we see Him, when the scales fall from our eyes, our response will be worship. They all had that response, though some still had to push through their struggle with doubt. Their worship prepared their hearts to accept the mission set before them. And the mission was this: Go and make disciples!

Why do you think Jesus prefaced His commission with these words: *"All authority in heaven and earth has been given to me. Therefore..."* (Matt. 28:18, 19)? Because they needed to know that they did not have to function with a slave mentality which would hinder their mission. They needed to know that the One with all authority, King of Kings on earth and in heaven, was the one sending them. They should go with the confidence of their royal status! And He ended the commission with further confidence building words: *"And surely I am with you always, to the very end of the age"* (Matt. 28:20).

I see a progression in these passages that I can relate to. First we listen and obey. This leads us to worship. If we have occasional doubts and fears, worship will help push through that. Worship will prepare our hearts to receive His call on our life. We will need to keep in mind that it is in His power and authority that we take that step of obedience to go, knowing that He will never leave us alone but will empower and equip us for extraordinary things.

Chapter 14
Slave Mentality

No matter how difficult things may get, God is there, calling us by name, reminding us who we are and Whose we are.

"But now, this is what the LORD says—
    he who created you, O Jacob,
    he who formed you, O Israel:
    "Fear not, for I have redeemed you;
    I have summoned you by name; you are mine.

"When you pass through the waters,
    I will be with you;
    and when you pass through the rivers,
    they will not sweep over you.
    When you walk through the fire,
    you will not be burned;
    the flames will not set you ablaze.

"For I am the LORD, your God,
    the Holy One of Israel, your Savior..."

(Isaiah 43:1-3)

Moses certainly passed through the waters, beginning with a slave basket as a boat. But God saw a bigger picture. And He sees a bigger picture in you, too. And He is calling you by name to take a look at that picture with Him.

But Moses still struggled with a slave mentality, even though he grew up in a palace with all the rights of a son at his beck and call. That slave mentality certainly showed through when, in anger over the harsh treatment of his lineage, he killed a man. And then, when found out, he ran for his life. The chosen, royal one was now a murdering fugitive, once again barely escaping a death sentence. But I wonder what would have happened if he had acted like the royalty that he was. What if he had tapped into all the privileges of being a royal son? He might have had the pull to have the man killed, his hands free of the blood guilt. But another truth was playing out.

True royalty does not come from earthly status. I know many that seem to have everything that this world could offer, yet as much as they try to rely on their earthly status, it just never measures up. I feel sorry for such people. They are truly still slaves trying to dress up as royalty so that no one will know how they really are. On the other hand, I know others that are true royalty, bought and paid for by the blood of the King, officially adopted into the royal family, yet they still act like slaves. They do not tap into all the riches of the King, their Heavenly Father.

Unfortunately, I can relate to both extremes, for I have been guilty of both. In the past, I have had moments of self-reliance, leaning on my own efforts, my own connections, and my own earthly significance. But, every time, this reliance left me empty. And there have been many times that I have lived with a slave mentality. Many times I have forgotten who I am, and Whose I am. And this tragic forgetfulness has left me feeling powerless and poor.

Missing God's Riches

I heard a story once about a homeless man that sat year after year on the streets of New York City, barely scraping by, living off the handouts of passersby. When he was found dead, obviously having perished due to the cold and exposure that he daily encountered, the police were shocked to find in his possession about $30,000 in cash. My husband's own grandfather lived in fear of overdrawing his account each time he wrote a check. However, at his death, we discovered $75,000 in his checking account.

If I should receive a million dollars placed into my checking account, what if I never wrote a check? What if I never took advantage of the gift? It would not change the fact that I was wealthy, but I certainly could still look and act like a pauper. And that is what Satan cunningly plans for us. He does not want us to know who we are and Whose we are. He does not want us to tap into the riches of God's ways. And he certainly does not want us to invest our riches in the lives of those around us, reaping a tremendous gain for the Kingdom of God. In fact, as long as he can keep us living with a slave mentality, we cannot reach our full royal status. Unless we encounter face to face the glory and love of the Lord, we will never be able to become all that God created us to be. But once we truly encounter Him, we will never be the same. However, we need to sharpen our memories because we quickly forget Him, His love, His power, His almighty dependability. Worship helps us remember.

Moses then settled in Midian among a group of shepherds. In the tradition of those days, shepherds were on the low rung of the social ladder. They were looked down upon and snubbed. So, Moses fell from a princely status and settled for mediocrity. He was content to leave his past behind him. He did not want to face his past, thus staying in that level of mediocrity.

Let me pause for a moment to say that I'm not knocking shepherds. God chose this same type of mediocre shepherd to be the first to hear the joyful proclamation of the birth of Christ, and Jesus Himself was called the Great Shepherd. Once again, this is evidence that God loves the common man and adores the ordinary. But He does not want us to stay ordinary. He wants to call us out of the ordinary and into His extraordinary plan. He does not want us to stay in the life of mediocrity. He has so much more for us than that. I am not referring to temporary earthly treasures, which moth and rust will destroy. I am referring to heavenly treasures—the pearl of great price, as the Bible puts it. I am talking about experiencing the kingdom of God on earth. And there is nothing mediocre about that. Some may be thinking that the kingdom of God will only be experienced in heaven. But why would Jesus have taught His disciples to pray, *"Your kingdom come, Your will be done in earth, as*

it is in heaven" (Matt. 6:10) if we could not experience to some
degree the kingdom of God here on earth?

Insecurities

Moses' calling came at a time when he least expected it. He
was 80 years old when he happened upon the burning bush.
And even though he was standing in front of a burning bush,
with the voice of God shouting out His glory, Moses still displayed his slave mentality. He said, *"Who am I, that I should go to
Pharaoh and bring the Israelites out of Egypt?"* (Ex. 3:11). God's reply
was, *"I will be with you"* (Ex. 3:12). Our confidence should not be
in ourselves, but in Him. Remember, God loves to use the ordinary to bring about the extraordinary. So, God took the very
symbol of Moses' mediocrity, his shepherd's staff and turned
it into a symbol of power, holiness and greatness. Once again,
the ordinary turned into the extraordinary. It was through this
ordinary staff with its ordinary owner that God displayed His
greatness through plagues and partings of the sea, and through
victorious battles.

Because Moses was ordinary, he, like many of us, dealt with
insecurity and self-awareness that held him back. We find the
first insecurity in Exodus 4:1: Moses answered, *"What if they
do not believe me or listen to me and say, 'The LORD did not appear to
you'?"* The second insecurity is found in Exodus 4:10: *"Moses said
to the LORD, 'O Lord, I have never been eloquent, neither in the past nor
since you have spoken to your servant. I am slow of speech and tongue.'"*

Of course, God was perfectly capable of healing him. Why
He did not, I don't know. Maybe Moses was unwilling to receive
healing. However, God did provide in spite of his weakness.

God provided Aaron. Remember, *"...all things work together for good to those who love God...."* (Rom. 8:28; NKJ). God is sovereign and mighty despite our resistance to His help.

But think about it: It was Aaron who led and allowed the people to sacrifice to the golden calf. And because of the disobedience, the people had to wander in the wilderness for 40 years. Aaron would have been destroyed along with all of the people if Moses had not stood in the gap, fasting and praying for 40 days and 40 nights. This act in itself points toward the Savior that was to come, as Jesus, too, fasted and prayed for 40 days and 40 nights in preparation for His ministry to provide a way of salvation, not only for the Israelites, but for the entire world. And the lesson for us is simply this: a lack of trust in God leads to hardship.

Your Mentality?

So let's push through to the practical: How are you (and I) like Moses? Do you have a slave mentality? Do words of self-hatred and self-condemnation fly through your mind on a regular basis? Do you feel unworthy to receive anything from the Lord? Do you find yourself in bondage to the cycle of sin-slavery: sin which leads to guilt which leads to promises that we can't keep which leads to more sin? Even Paul dealt with that in Romans 7:14-25:

> *"We know that the law is spiritual; but I am unspiritual, sold as a slave to sin. I do not understand what I do. For what I want to do I do not do, but what I hate I do. And if I do what I do not want to do, I agree that the law is good. As it is, it is no longer I myself who do*

it, but it is sin living in me. I know that nothing good lives in me, that is, in my sinful nature. For I have the desire to do what is good, but I cannot carry it out. For what I do is not the good I want to do; no, the evil I do not want to do—this I keep on doing. Now if I do what I do not want to do, it is no longer I who do it, but it is sin living in me that does it.

"So I find this law at work: When I want to do good, evil is right there with me. For in my inner being I delight in God's law; but I see another law at work in the members of my body, waging war against the law of my mind and making me a prisoner of the law of sin at work within my members. What a wretched man I am! Who will rescue me from this body of death? Thanks be to God—through Jesus Christ our Lord!"

But there is good news which Paul found, which I found and which you, too, can find: Jesus came to set the captives free! In His very first sermon, Jesus stood up and proclaimed the fulfillment of prophesy found in Isaiah 61:1-3:

"The Spirit of the Sovereign LORD is on me,
because the LORD has anointed me
to preach good news to the poor.
He has sent me to bind up the brokenhearted,
to proclaim freedom for the captives
and release from darkness for the prisoners,
to proclaim the year of the LORD's favor
and the day of vengeance of our God,
to comfort all who mourn,

and provide for those who grieve in Zion—
to bestow on them a crown of beauty
instead of ashes,
the oil of gladness
instead of mourning,
and a garment of praise
instead of a spirit of despair.
They will be called oaks of righteousness,
a planting of the LORD
for the display of his splendor."

Through the shed blood of Jesus, we can be released from the slavery of sin.

Do you, like Moses, run and hide from your past mistakes? The truth is that your past is a part of you and it will catch up with you. The only way to deal with it is looking at it squarely. In Ephesians six, we are told about the wonderful armor of God that we are each given: the breastplate of righteousness, the helmet of salvation, the belt of truth, the shoes of peace, the shield of faith and the sword of the Spirit which is the Word of God. Each piece of armor is ours to take and wear and use so that we can stand firm. However, think for a moment about the placement of the pieces of armor—they are all on the front. If we don't face our sin, our fears, our anger and our past, we can get hit from behind.

Moses eventually overcame his past, his slave mentality, and his life of mediocrity when he stopped running. He did not run from the voice of God in the burning bush. He stopped, stood face to face with God and took off his running sandals, because he knew he was standing on holy ground. I'm sure he was terribly afraid, but after he quit running and saw God for who He really is, he craved that presence. Later, he spent much time in the Tent of Meeting where the presence of God was the strongest; and once, he begged to see the full glory of God. It was said of Moses that he talked with God as a friend. That could only take place when he quit running and began to allow the Great Physician to heal his past. Jesus can do the same for you, if you will let Him.

Chapter 15

A Life of Worship

The Westminster catechism says that the chief end of man is to glorify God and enjoy Him forever. As our ultimate purpose, glorifying God brings us deep joy. On earth, we are each assigned different means of glorifying Him. But the preparation for the assignment is the same for all of us: worship, true heartfelt worship. More than the good ole' "go to church on Sunday and Wednesday night and that's it" kind of worship. I'm talking personal, face-to-face realization that He is an extraordinary God who deserves more than we could ever offer Him, but who is somehow pleased with a heart that simply acknowledges and loves Him.

We can worship corporately, such as during Bible Study or a Sunday church service, but we must also worship privately. We can worship with prayer and praises. We can worship with singing. We can worship by reading and meditating and memorizing and remembering God's Word. And we can worship Him by reaching out to others. Our good deeds are an act of worship.

Keith Green wrote a beautiful song with the following words: "Make my life a prayer to You." Every action and word of our lives can be an act of worship. And this happens through complete surrender to Him.

The Throne of Thrones

We see that God called Moses and Joshua to a mighty purpose. But although they did not take the assignment lightly, they did not feel equipped in their own abilities to fulfill the assignment. So they worshipped in good times and bad times and in joy and in sorrow. Moses led the people in worship through all the years of wandering in the desert. Exodus 33:7 says, *"Moses used to take a tent and pitch it outside the camp some distance away, calling it the 'tent of meeting'."* I believe that the tent of meeting was pitched outside the camp for several reasons.

First of all, we cannot forget the holiness of God. We must realize that though we are able to "come boldly to the throne of grace" through Jesus, it is still a throne. A throne calls for reverence, attention, and acknowledgement of its superiority. And we are not just talking about any old throne. This is the throne of all thrones, holding the presence of the King of all Kings and Lord of all Lords. All earthly thrones will fall and come to naught. And yet we pay homage to these temporary thrones. How much more should we come with awe, diligence, respect and reverence to the eternal throne? Our true worship brings us to a front row seat before the eternal throne. Our prayers and praises thrust us forward to His mighty feet, propped up on the footstool of the earth.

Worship: Sweet-Smelling Incense for the Lord

I once attended a worship conference at a large church in the Chicago area. One night we attended a worship service with thousands of people. The people were of one accord praying and praising. My heart was filled to overflowing and my desire to please the Lord grew stronger. At one point, I looked around at the believers gathered together, and I prayed, "Lord, are you pleased with our worship? Are you pleased, Lord?" Suddenly a picture formed in my imagination: Jesus rose to his feet from the throne with outstretched arms. And then He brought His arms forward towards His face in a grand sweeping motion, as if He smelled something divine. The picture in my imagination brought tears to my eyes, and joy to my soul; and I felt a true peace that our worship was indeed pleasing to Him.

A few days later, back at my home, I was reading my Bible and came across the following verses:

"Then I saw in the right hand of him who sat on the throne a scroll with writing on both sides and sealed with seven seals. And I saw a mighty angel proclaiming in a loud voice, 'Who is worthy to break the seals and open the scroll?' But no one in heaven or on earth or under the earth could open the scroll or even look inside it. I wept and wept because no one was found who was worthy to open the scroll or look inside. Then one of the elders said to me, 'Do not weep! See, the Lion of the tribe of Judah, the Root of David, has triumphed. He is able to open the scroll and its seven seals.'

"Then I saw a Lamb, looking as if it had been slain, standing in the center of the throne, encircled by the four living creatures and the elders.

He had seven horns and seven eyes, which are the seven spirits of God
sent out into all the earth. He came and took the scroll from the right
hand of him who sat on the throne. And when he had taken it, the
four living creatures and the twenty four elders fell down before the
Lamb. Each one had a harp and they were holding golden bowls full
of incense, which are the prayers of the saints. And they sang a new
song:
'You are worthy to take the scroll and to open its seals, because you were
slain, and with your blood you purchased men for God from every tribe
and language and people and nation. You have made them to be a
kingdom and priests to serve our God, and they will reign on the
earth."

(Revelation 5:1-10)

You see, our true worship is sweet smelling aroma to the
Lord. And our praises and prayers move heaven and change
earth. And as we have just read, we are called to be a kingdom
and priests to serve our God. We are called to leave our slave
mentality behind, and walk as royalty.

"But you are a chosen people, a royal priesthood, a holy nation, a people
belonging to God, that you may declare the praises of him who called
you out of darkness into his wonderful light."

(1 Peter 2:9)

Effort and Obedience
Another reason that I believe the tent of meeting was placed
outside the camp is because true worship requires effort and
obedience on our part. True worship is not always convenient,
and is often painful because it strips us of false pride, false

humility and false strength. We can't enter true worship without being totally aware of our inadequacies. But true worship heightens our awareness of His abundant adequacies. Second Timothy 1:11-13 says, *"For I know whom I have believed, and am persuaded that He is able to keep that which I have committed to Him against that day"* (KJV). Paul wrote these words in the midst of a discussion of his suffering. This kind of confidence, faith and patience come from the knowledge, peace and assurance gained from our personal times of true worship.

Holy Hush

The tent of meeting was a place of worship. It was a place where Moses could go to be in the presence of God. God met him there. We see evidence that God was with Moses always, but when he was in the tent of meeting it was a divine set-apart time. We need that divine time each day as well. My friend, Kelli, calls it a holy hush. Psalm 46:10 says, *"Be still and know that I am God."* This holy hush prepares us for our purpose: to be participants in the extraordinary.

> *"And whenever Moses went out to the tent, all the people rose and stood at the entrances to their tents watching Moses until he entered the tent. As Moses went into the tent, the pillar of cloud would come down and stay at the entrance, while the Lord spoke with Moses. Whenever the people saw the pillar of cloud standing at the entrance to the tent, they all stood and worshiped each at the entrance to his tent."*
>
> (Exodus 33:8-10)

Moses may have been oblivious to others watching his sincere worship, but they did. And so do others watch us, as believers. His sincere worship affected others, causing them to rise up and stand at the entrance of their own tents. It caused others to stop what they were doing and take notice. But Moses couldn't see them. He just saw God. The pillar of cloud would come down and stay at the entrance, blocking Moses' view of others.

True worship does the same for us. When we worship, in spirit and in truth, then our view of others is blocked out, even if only temporarily. Suddenly, we have an audience of One; or rather we are the observer of a one-on-one display of magnificent glory. And we are changed. But we are not the only ones changed. We also see in those verses that when the cloud, which was the presence of the Lord, descended, when true worship began, the focus was no longer on Moses. The focus and glory was God's alone.

"They all stood and worshiped each at the entrance to his tent."
(Exodus 33:10)

They did not go to the tent of meeting to worship, but seeing Moses' true worship did affect change in the whole camp. So it is with us. We may never see the extent of effect that our true worship has on others this side of heaven. But it affects the thread of the tapestry being woven all around us. It may begin the weaving of a holy tapestry in the hearts of others. But that is not why we worship. That is just a wonderful consequence of worship.

We worship because we realize Who God is. When we begin to get even a glimpse of that, the knowledge alone demands a response. The response will be different in different people.

Some will pray, some will cry, some will laugh, and some will raise their hands. Some will sit quietly and meditate in their heart. God has made so many different personalities; it makes sense to me that the response would be different in each one, personalized between us and God. But the common factor is that a change of heart occurs in the midst of true worship.

Friendship With God

"The Lord would speak to Moses face to face, as a man speaks with his friend." (Exodus 33:11)

It is during our times of worship that intimacy in our friendship with God grows and develops. Our closest friends are the ones that we have spent much time with, and in whom we confide. In the same way, time spent in worship, both private and corporate, is the means of developing a best-friend status with the King of Kings.

As leader, Moses would then return to the camp, to the outside world. We can't stay in the tent of meeting all day, every day. We do have work to do. God has given us an assignment, a purpose, which will require entering the outside world. But we are called to be in the world but not a part of the world. True worship gives us the strength to engage in the world, but not to be stained by it. Daily worship equips us for our daily assignments, which God graciously entrusts to each of us. Consistent worship equips us to look and act like a friend of God.

There are, however, seasons of our life that God calls us to take time away and come apart from the world. There will be seasons that you need to spend more concentrated time with God, because He is preparing you for something new and special and extraordinary.

> "…but his young aide, Joshua, son of Nun, did not leave the tent."
>
> (Exodus 33:11)

Joshua did not yet know that God would call him to the mighty task of leading the people into the Promised Land. He did not yet know that he, an ordinary man, would be called to an extraordinary assignment. All he knew at that point was that he had to be near God. This season of separation from the rest of the camp was preparation for the great task ahead. I, too, have had times like that. I have, at times, been called to resist all urges of busyness, no matter how "good" the busyness is. And I have found that almost always, those times of being called aside for long periods of time in His presence result in me being equipped for a new God-assigned task.

I may not even understand that He is preparing me for something. I simply must be obedient when He calls me to clear the calendar. There are times that I was commanded to say no to everything in my life. It did not even make sense to me, but if I was disobedient, I felt the rebuke of the Lord. Not only that, I felt that His hand of favor was not on the task I was trying to complete, and it caused major stress for me, and poor results for others.

Whether it is a season of intense worship or simply daily time with the Lord, worship is crucial for our lives and our mission. When we learn to truly worship, we can't forget. We praise Him and worship Him because of who He is, not because of what He has done. The fact that He is God is enough knowledge for us to continually praise Him. I learned this lesson from a young Shuar Indian boy in Ecuador.

Praise in The Midst of The Storm

My husband and I were on a three-month mission trip to Ecuador. Mont was a fourth-year medical student, and he was doing a foreign internship at a remote hospital in Shell Mera. This hospital was the last stop before the jungle stretched towards Peru. There were remote Indian villages scattered throughout the jungle, but they could not be reached by car—only by plane or on foot. Mission Aviation Fellowship was stationed in Shell Mera, and the pilots did a wonderful job of flying patients in and out, often in emergency situations. One such situation occurred right before dusk on an April evening in 1992. An emergency call came forth over the radio that a young boy, a Shuar Indian, had been bitten by a snake. Because of the remote location of the village, the pilots were unable to get to the boy before dark. Flying had to take place during the daylight hours because the "airstrips" were only grassy areas cleared of trees. The absence of lights in the village and on the airstrip made it impossible to land, much less find the village in the dark. Word was sent back by radio transmission that a pilot would come for the boy at the first light of dawn, and that the missionaries would be in prayer.

Early the next morning the pilots took off, anxious to see how bad the situation was. They brought the boy to the hospital and the doctors immediately took him to surgery to try to stop the poison. Unfortunately, it was unsuccessful. They tried two more surgeries, but ultimately were forced to amputate the boy's leg in order to save his life. Mont had assisted in two of the surgeries and I had diligently prayed for his leg to be saved. We contemplated the implications of a jungle boy with one leg. It would be devastating enough for any child, but for a child who lived in a hut, dependent on his own physical abilities to survive in the jungle, the implications were enormous; not to mention all of the superstitions that arose among the Indians concerning anyone who was not "whole" or "complete".

With heavy hearts, Mont and I made our way down the path to the hospital. We were determined to find a way to offer comfort to the boy and his family. When we arrived at the hospital room, we heard beautiful voices coming from within. We paused at the door and listened. Then we gently knocked and opened the door. The boy and his family were in a time of worship and praise. They had invited other patients to their room and were singing praises and songs of thanksgiving to their Creator. You see, they were Christians. In fact, they were very involved in the translation of the Old Testament into their Shuar language. And at that moment, when I expected tears and mourning and fears of the future, I saw worship. I saw praise. I saw trust in a way that I had never had to experience. And it was beautiful. They had found completeness and wholeness already, regardless of their circumstances. They praised and worshiped God because He is God.

And, as I saw their faces, I realized that the worship had lifted their chains of worry, fear and despair. Yes, there were still obstacles to deal with, but that time of worship was lifting them above the situation. They were finding strength to endure. And, as true worship always brings perspective change, their eyes saw hope and light, and the despair and darkness fled.

And so our true worship does the same. It brings perspective change. And it brings hope and light to every dark situation. True worship is preparation for our ordinary hearts to be ready for God's extraordinary plans. Once again, we see how important it is to Reach Up to God through true worship, which prepares us for our particular mission to Reach Out to Others, all the while Remembering to give all the glory to Him!

Chapter 16
Remember

My fourth child, Troy, was off to school for the first time. I was surprised at what a hard time I had with that. After all, I had endured the trauma of the first three of my children heading off to school. You would think that I would be used to it, even a little excited about it, by now. But I wasn't. I kept wondering if I had made the best use of the time that I had had with him before he ended up being with others more hours of the day than with me. I wanted to know that our sweet relationship was solid enough. Yes, I expected change, but I hoped that that special bond would not leave.

One day, when I picked him up from school, he reached into his backpack and showed me a pecan that he had found lying on the ground under a pecan tree on the playground. I told him how much I loved pecans. They remind me of going to my grandparents' house when I was a little girl. Their three-acre yard was filled with pecan trees. And we spent many hours gathering boxes full of pecans. They even had a special nut-cracker that they allowed us to use.

Troy listened patiently and quietly while I reminisced, then continued telling me about his school day. I figured my words were going in one ear and out the other. The next day, and the next, and the next, and for many days after, Troy would bring me pecans. Soon, his backpack was so heavy with these treasures that I had to gently encourage him to spend his recess time playing soccer or climbing on the playground equipment. But secretly, those days of pecan-gathering by my precious son brought joy to my heart.

The reason that those pecans were so special to me was because he remembered me. I know that sounds like an insecure mom, but I know the reality of friends and studies and teachers—he could go a whole day and not think of me. But when he saw the pecans, he remembered his mom! That meant so much to me. And then I thought: How must our Heavenly Father feel when the busyness of our lives makes us forget Him, who has done so much for us? That is what Stones of Remembrance are all about.

The Pain of Being Forgotten

To be remembered evokes a joy to our souls that is a matchless feeling. It can come in big or small ways: the special gift on your anniversary; the phone call from a long-distance friend; the card on your birthday, when you thought no one remembered. It doesn't even matter what action the remembrance brings, it is simply the fact that you were the object of remembrance.

And what of the times that we are not remembered? What about forgotten birthdays or when someone you thought that you knew well does not recognize you? It inflicts us with pain and self-doubt that wounds our souls. I have been on the receiving end and inflicting end of both remembering and forgetting.

I once was in a large mall in Memphis, TN. I was very tired, almost asleep in fact, as I sat on a bench waiting for a particular store to open. As the storekeeper finally opened the doors, I entered with my mind still in a fog. The storekeeper did a double-take and then spoke to me, saying, "Hello, Sara, how are you?" I looked up and saw a face that I recognized. The fog in my brain and the years that had passed since I had seen the face prevented me from remembering who she was, or from where I knew her. I was not alert enough to hide my forgetfulness, so I honestly said, "I'm so sorry. I know we know each other, but I can't remember from where." The look on her face showed surprise and hurt. She simply said, "We were in school together." I immediately remembered, but the damage was done. I quickly apologized and tried to explain how many different cities that I had lived in since then, but I saw that I had wounded her, and it was too late to take it back. I quickly paid for the item that I had come for, and left with a sick feeling in my stomach. I was terribly disheartened when several years later she did not show up for our class reunion. I have prayed for her that my blunder would not cause her self-doubt in any way, and that if it had, that that area of her life would be healed.

On the other hand, I remember a time when as a single Christian woman my roommate and I had taken notice of a particular single young man. We knew him to be a committed Christian with a likeable personality, and to top it off, he was pleasing to the eye. We lived in separate cities, but were going to his city for a weekend visit, and we talked about and hoped to run into him while we were there. We were at a picnic given for single adults by a local church, and sure enough we spotted the man that we had talked about for several weeks. We found ourselves talking to a mutual friend when he walked up. Our mutual friend included him in our circle of conversation, saying, "Oh, you remember Sara and Kelli, don't you?" His reply stunned us both. "No, I don't think we have met before." It took some intense Scripture-based self-talk to keep that comment from causing insecurity and doubt.

He Will Not Forget

I also remember a time when I discovered the loyalty and remembrance that my God has for me and all of His Children. I had long had the habit of writing Scripture passages on slips of paper and taking them with me in my pocket or purse. When I was a junior in college, I felt called to leave my present college and attend another one so that I could work with a youth group in Memphis, TN. This calling came at a time that seemed very unlikely. I was at the height of my college career. Things were going very well at my present college: my grades were very good, I had many precious friendships, I was leading Bible studies, and I had just been crowned homecoming queen. Yet, I could not shake the feeling that I needed to leave for a season. I knew that I would return to graduate there, but I wondered if I would still have a "place" when I returned. I knew I just had to trust the Lord to take care of that, so I proceeded in moving. As I was unpacking in my new home, I came across one of those many slips of paper. When I read it, I couldn't remember ever having read it before, much less having written it down. Yet, there it was in my own handwriting. I read it and re-read it over and over. The verse said:

"Can a mother forget the baby at her breast and have no compassion on the child she has borne? Though she may forget, I will not forget you! See, I have engraved you on the palms of my hands."

(Isaiah 49:15-16)

A great peace swept over me, and joyful tears began to stream down my face. Others may forget me, but He will not! The reminder is on his nail-scarred hands—a special engraving; a symbol of remembrance. He will not forget me! What security that brings!

But what of my remembrance of Him? So often I forget Him. I forget to include Him in my decision-making. I forget to thank Him for His innumerable blessings. I forget to pray and to read His Word. I forget to believe Him, despite the many times that He has proven His love for me. How must that make God feel when we forget?

Joshua seemed to take great pains to remember, spending much time in worship at the temple. Sincere and consistent worship definitely helps to spark our memory, and is a safeguard against forgetfulness. But Joshua was ordinary. God knew that this ordinary status could cause him to forget his extraordinary calling and his extraordinary God. He also knew that in order for Joshua to fulfill and complete his extraordinary calling, he must remember. In Exodus 17:8-15, we read the following account:

"The Amalekites came and attacked the Israelites at Rephidim. Moses said to Joshua, 'Choose some of our men and go out to fight the Amalekites. Tomorrow I will stand on top of the hill with the staff of God in my hands.'

"So Joshua fought the Amalekites as Moses had ordered, and Moses, Aaron and Hur went to the top of the hill. As long as Moses held up his hands, the Israelites were winning, but whenever he lowered his hands, the Amalekites were winning. When Moses' hands grew tired, they took a stone and put it under him and he sat on it. Aaron and Hur held his hands up—one on one side, one on the other—so that his hands remained steady till sunset. So Joshua overcame the Amalekite army with the sword.

"Then the Lord said to Moses, 'Write this on a scroll as something to be remembered and make sure that Joshua hears it, because I will completely blot out the memory of Amalek from under heaven.' Moses built an altar and called it The Lord is Banner [Jehovah Nissi]. He said, 'For hands were lifted up to the throne of the Lord. The Lord will be at war against the Amalekites from generation to generation.'"

(Exodus 17:8-16)

God was the most important character in this story! All the secondary characters had equally important parts with a role to play. But, everyone had to depend on each other to have victory.

And then the Lord had some strict instructions for them. He told Moses to write down the details of this victory so that they would remember. And he added: *"and make sure Joshua hears it"* (Ex. 17:14). God wanted Moses to make sure Joshua heard all of the details of battle because He knew what the future held for Joshua. He knew how He would use Joshua to finally lead the people into the Promised Land. He knew that Joshua would face these enemies again. He knew that this was an extraordinary job, and He knew that Joshua was ordinary. Joshua needed to remember in order to have the courage and strength to face the days ahead.

So Moses showed the scroll to Joshua and he did something else: He built an altar. In those days, building an altar meant gathering stones. And that is what I have been doing in this book: gathering my own precious stones of remembrance and sharing them with you.

Seasons
of
Remembering

Chapter 17
Summer

When I began writing this book a couple of years ago, I was writing it for my children. I wanted to make sure that I remembered to tell them about the many powerful ways that God has shown Himself mighty on my behalf. This book was birthed in my big green chair, where I sat daily to spend time with my Lord. In that chair, I read the holy Word of God, the living Word which cuts through my sin, my selfishness, and this world's deceitfulness, and offers the only truth, hope and peace.

From my big green chair I can look out the window and see a grove of tall trees. Each season, as I looked out at those trees, I learned something fresh and new.

"The heavens declare the glory of God; the skies proclaim the work of his hands. Day after day they pour forth speech; night after night they display knowledge...." (Psalm 19:1-2)

Throughout the springtime I watched the trees gradually obtain more and more leaves, until the summer broke forth in all the fullness of a completed work. During the summer months, I looked out my window and I saw the leaves of those trees all lush and green. I love to watch when a gentle wind breaks through the heat and humidity. It starts at the top of the tree, where the leaves are fewer and more scattered. But, as the leaves at the top get caught up in the blowing wind, others begin to sway as well. The movement is almost contagious! Within a short amount of time the whole tree, as well as the neighboring trees are swaying together in perfect unity.

It reminds me of the Body of Christ, the church as a whole. Different trees, different leaves, but how beautiful when we sway together, enjoying the rushing wind of the Holy Spirit. Often it starts at the top. The Christian leaders play such a role in guiding the other believers. But each leaf feels the wind, just as each person in the Body of Christ can experience the work of the Holy Spirit in their individual lives.

How beautiful it is when there is unity in the Body; all its unique members with different functions. Some members in the Body are very different from me, but I have found through the years that I can learn many things from many different kinds of people. Of course, the unity can only come from those who are truly a part of the Body. We are warned in Scripture not to be *"unequally yoked"* (2 Cor. 6:14). But even if we can't be unified with an unbeliever, we certainly can treat them in a loving manner. In fact, we are commanded to love.

A couple of years ago I was listening to my husband and two of his friends share before our church about their recent mission trip to China. One of the friends made a reference to "other wicked religions". A dear friend of mine leaned over and whispered, "Do you believe that?" I felt uncomfortable with the question, but nodded in the affirmative. But it bothered me. I felt the need to explain my answer further, so I wrote the following in an email:

Hey! Thanks for coming last night. It meant a lot to both me and Mont! Something that has been on my mind since then....

You asked me if I agreed when Jim referred to the "wickedness" of the other religions. I said I did. I wanted to clarify that a bit. You probably haven't thought twice about that, but humor me for a minute! First, I agreed because I know the heart from which Jim said that. He said that from a heart that loves our God as the only true God. He said that from a heart that loves people who don't know the only true God. He said that from a heart that would spend his vacation time and money and his 40th birthday away from his family in order to build pigpens for the very people who follow this "wicked" religion. In other words, the words were not meant for the followers of this religion, but for the religion itself. The followers of this religion are simply lost. No more lost than I was before I truly came to have an understanding and love for Jesus. It seems very strong to say "wicked," however, anything apart from Christ is wicked, even me before I came to Him. Now, I'm not; but that is not because of any good works or good moral choices that I have done, but because of what Jesus has done for me. That is why Jesus came. It is with great love and compassion that we talk of the wickedness of other religions. Some are wrong and violent; some are more moral and "good". The more moral and "good" ones may make this world a bit more bearable, but that does not make them true or right. Some people think that we all have the same god, just called by different names, but that totally goes against what the Bible says. So that is why we go on mission trips, because we want all to know the one true God, the only eternal God. I don't know exactly how God does it, being totally just and totally loving. He is both. I don't have to worry about that, I trust who He is. I do believe that we have to do our part in what he calls us to do to lead others in our sphere of influence to the one true God.

Anyway, thanks for letting me get my thoughts together on that. I did not want you to misinterpret what I said. I love you! Sara

The Bible says of Jesus that *"Salvation is found in no one else, for there is no other name under heaven given to men by which we must be saved"* (Acts 4:12).

It also says in Philippians 2:5-10:

"Your attitude should be the same as that of Christ Jesus: Who, being in very nature God, did not consider equality something to be grasped, but made himself nothing, taking the very nature of a servant, being made in human likeness. And being found in appearance as a man, he humbled himself and he came obedient to death—even death on a cross! Therefore God exalted him to the highest place and gave him the name that is above every name, that at the name of Jesus every knee should bow, in heaven and on earth and under the earth, and every tongue confess that Jesus Christ is Lord, to the glory of God the Father."

We will not all see things in exactly the same way, but God has given us His Word to be a guide for unity. We cannot compromise truth, but we cannot be arrogant with our truth either. How will the lost world know if we do not speak the truth in love? And why would they even want to know about our faith if all they see in us is dissension, pettiness and bitterness?

We must ask the Lord to increase the fruit of His Holy Spirit in our lives. Empowered by the Spirit let us demostrate "...*love, joy, peace, patience, kindness, goodness, faithfulness, gentleness, and self-control...*" (Gal. 5:22) toward unbelievers in our world, and toward our brothers and sisters in Christ. St. Augustine said, "In essentials, unity. In non-essentials, diversity. In all things, charity."xiii May God help us to accept and show consistent respect to Christ followers in all denominations and non-denominational groups. We are the Family of God.

Kingdom Perspective

My husband and I have been on several mission trips to China. We have served and worshipped with hundreds of beautiful believers there, but many of them have life struggles that are quite different from those I face in America. Both culturally and officially, China is opposed to the "religion" of Christianity. Although much of this hostility is based on long-distant abuses by Christian Westerners, ignorance and myth, many Chinese believers live with the constant threat of public embarrassment, professional censorship, and fines. Although the concept of religious freedom is slowly growing, some Christians face the possibility of imprisonment and even death, all because they are commited to love and serve Jesus.

I realize that Chinese Christians and churches have their own share of temptations and struggles, but I can't believe that they battle the problem of petty divisions in the same way that we do in America. The primary distinctions are not made about what type of Christian you are, as in denominations, but about whether you are a Christian at all. They have more important things to deal with.

"Paul" is a dear South Korean missionary who is is serving the lost in Asia. We know him as Paul, but that is not his name. My husband has known him for several years, and has no idea what his real name is. Christian workers in many places in the world often take on different names in order to protect their ministries, coworkers and families. Imagine living in a place where you feel the need to use a pseudonym because of the risk of Christian persecution?

While he was visiting our church in Tupelo, Paul told the story of a young Christian that he met in North Korea, one of the most spiritually dark and oppressed places on this earth. To become a Christian in North Korea is to choose a deadly path. Yet the gospel cannot be stopped, because it is absolutely true and the only hope of this world. Once Paul finally arrived in North Korea, a rare opportunity, he sat in his hotel wondering how he would be able to witness for Christ. He had to be very careful about sharing his faith, for all foreigners are watched in every way imaginable. So day after day Paul walked back and forth down the street in front of his hotel. As he walked, he silently prayed that the Holy Spirit would lead him to just one Christian to encourage. Miraculously that happened. One day Paul met a young North Korean man who was, indeed, a Christian.

The young believer had become a Christian when he began to read a portion of God's Word that had been smuggled into

North Korea. He believed that he was the only Christian in the whole city. The young Korean was starving in many ways. The oppressive government made life difficult; food was hard to find. But he was also starving for Christian fellowship. Paul had to leave the country, but he felt that the Lord would allow him to return. As he was leaving, he asked the young man, "What can I bring you when I return?" Paul expected him to ask for rice or other physical necessities, but the young man replied tearfully that there were only two things that he wanted in this life. The first thing he wanted was to be baptized. Paul was joyfully able to accommodate that request. The second thing he wanted was an opportunity. You see, he had read something about the Christian principal of tithing, but he didn't have a church or Christian group to which he could give his offering. Amazingly, he had been saving 10% of his meager income; waiting on the day that he would have the privilege to honor God by giving to the Lord's work. The young North Korean brother tearfully requested that Paul would give his tithe to a church.

How many churches have to beg its members to give? And here was a young, starving Christian, living in one of the most impoverished nations of the world, who longed to give his tithe to a fellowship of believers. Mont has said many times that he first went to China feeling sorry for the Christians living there, and he came home feeling sorry for us here.

Chapter 18
Autumn and Winter

When I sit in my big green chair in the fall of the year, I look out my window and watch the trees in the cool autumn air. I see the death of their leaves and know that this death of self produces an indescribable beauty of yellow, red, green and brown, all mixed together for a glorious vision of what our own lives could be if only we, too, would die to self. If only we would quit striving so hard to have and gain and simply be and become. If only we would remember that true freedom, for ourselves and for those we love, only comes through sacrifice and death. History proves that great, lasting things come only through death, be it our great country, or the salvation of our souls exemplified in the great, sacrificial death of our only Savior, Jesus. If only we could realize that all the while this death of self produces seed for the future. And this seed comes forth from an extraordinary God through the lives of ordinary people.

"I have been crucified with Christ and I no longer live, but Christ lives in me. The life I live in the body, I live by faith in the Son of God, who loved me and gave himself up for me".   (Galatians 2:20)

To be crucified means to die. We can't truly live the abundant life that Christ offers us until we die to our old self. That is why Christians refer to being "born again". The media at times has made that term seem a little weird, but I have to tell you that I am a "born again" Christian. I am not who I was before. And the truth is there is a constant struggle within myself to continually die to self and my selfish plans. But it is only when we die to self that we can see the extraordinary work of God in our ordinary lives. As we learned from our study of Esther, these can be described as "for such a time as this moments". We will never play our God-given role in those moments until we learn to daily die to ourselves, and live for Christ.

A "for such a time as this" moment came to my husband one afternoon during a busy day of clinic. He came into the examination room to see the next patient, took one look at the patient and asked the man who had accompanied the patient to come out into the hallway. He said, "Sir, this man is about to die. Why did you bring him here instead of the Emergency Room?" The man was the chaplain at the hospice center, and had brought the man to Mont's clinic upon the prompting of the Holy Spirit.

Mont returned to the examination room and sat down beside the patient, and said, "Sir, I know that you must understand that your time left on this earth is very short. I need to ask you a hard question. Do you know where you will spend eternity?"

The man could not speak because the cancer had taken his vocal cords, but he slowly shook his head, "No". Mont explained to the man that his past did not matter, and that Jesus came to be his Savior, and to provide a way to eternal and abundant life. Mont asked the man if he had ever asked Jesus to be his Lord and Savior. Once again, the man shook his head, "No". Mont asked a third question to the man. "Do you want to pray and receive Jesus as your Lord and Savior?" This time the man nodded an affirmative "Yes!" Mont then led the patient in the prayer of salvation, as the chaplain and Mont's nurse all rejoiced.

Afterwards, Mont left the room for a moment, returning five minutes later. When he walked back into the examination room, he saw that the man's earthly life had ended and his eternal life had begun. For such a time as this! Mont was an ordinary man being used by an extraordinary God. Dying to self, just like the autumn leaves, gives us divine opportunities to sow seeds of kindness and joy, comfort and friendship, truth and hope. Of course, before the seed bursts forth in full bloom of newness and growth, it often must rest in the cold of winter.

Winter

I was sitting in my big green chair during the winter and looked out the window at the barrenness in the trees. During the winter, it is hard to remember the more beautiful seasons. The barrenness of the trees often reminds me of those undeniable times that life brings a lonely, cold season. During those seasons of life, time seems to drag by. Often longing for reprieve from the heaviness, we try to self-medicate, filling ourselves with remedies that could never truly heal. We must remember that, as uncomfortable as these times may be, the Great Physician longs to use them for a grand purpose and deep healing.

> *"I will give you the treasures of darkness,*
>   *riches stored in secret places,*
>   *so that you may know that I am the LORD,*
>   *the God of Israel, who summons you by name."*
>
> (Isaiah 45:3)

Oh that I could remember the seed, lying dormant in the midst of the coldness and darkness. In these winter times of life, we are given the privilege of "walking by faith, not by sight". My mother used to tell me: "When you are having a hard time, God is preparing you for a blessing. Look for the blessing!" And she was right. There have been many winter days in my life. But my God has never failed me. Even if I don't feel it, or see evidence of it, I make myself remember that He says, *"I will never leave you, nor forsake you"* (Heb. 13:5; NKJ). That is a promise, a covenant made by the God who keeps His promises, always, forever, even when I don't understand, feel, or see it. For that is what faith really is: *"being sure of what we hope for and certain of what we do not see"* (Heb. 11:1). We can be sure because He is faithful to us, even when we are not.

Hebrews 10:23 says, *"Let us hold unswervingly to the hope we profess, for He who promised is faithful."* Holding unswerving to what we know and believe to be true is much like how I ride a roller coaster. I am not like those brave souls who lift both hands in the air, enjoying the rush of the experience. I tend to look at the structure too carefully. How on earth can those little rails really hold me up when I am upside down?! So I approach the ride with both hands holding "unswervingly" to the rail and with my feet planted solidly on the floor of the car. Then I can enjoy the wind and the thrill of the ride. But it takes an effort on my part to hold on. Joshua told the people just before he died: *"...hold fast to the Lord your God..."* (Josh. 23:8).

Faith

During one particular season of my life, the Lord kept taking me over and over to Hebrews 11. It was the assigned reading in my Bible studies; my Bible would happen to open there when I flipped through the pages; and it seemed that every sermon that I heard revolved around that particular passage. Once, I left the worship service, having heard another sermon which referred to Hebrews 11, to go feed my newborn son, Joshua. Since we were meeting in an old warehouse at the time, the only "Nursing Mother's Room" was in the children director's office. As I sat in her chair, I looked around the room perusing the books and literature on her bookshelf. Suddenly, three shelves down, I noticed a large curriculum box with neon green lettering which read, "Hebrews 11".

At that point I was a bit nervous. Why was God speaking so loudly to me about faith? Was something going to take place in my future that would require an added measure of faith? But as soon as those thoughts would appear, I would *"take every thought captive to the obedience of Christ, casting down imaginations and destroying speculations, and every high thing that exalts itself against the knowledge of God."* (2 Cor. 10: 4-6) I refused to fear. But it took a lot of remembering that I have an extraordinary God who loves me and blesses me abundantly. So I read, and reread Hebrews 11 over and over and over again. I learned many things, but the things in particular that had an "ah-hah!" affect on me were the following passages:

> *"Now faith is being sure of what we hope for and certain of what we do not see. This is what the ancients were commended for."*
>
> (Hebrews 11:1, 2)

Being sure and certain, even when our earthly eyes can't see clearly takes discipline in our thoughts and actions. We must take our thoughts captive and resist Satan's attempt to cause doubt and confusion. God's Word assures us that if we resist Satan, he must flee from us (James 4:7). All because the authority that comes to us when we become children of the King of Kings! Remember who you are! How wonderful it will be one day to hear those precious words from our Lord, *"Well done, my good and faithful servant..."* (Matt. 25:23)—all because we simply believed.

> *"And without faith it is impossible to please God, because anyone who comes to him must believe that he exists and that he rewards those who earnestly seek him."*
>
> (Hebrews 11:6)

I have five children. I see in them the universal characteristic of children, young or old, towards their fathers. Even though they are tempted to act in unpleasing ways at times, deep down they want to please their parents. We all want that parental approval, especially from our fathers. We want to hear in our souls our fathers say through words and actions: "I am pleased with you. I like and love you. You are mine, and I am so proud of you!"

In the same way, deep down, we want to please our Heavenly Father. It is an innate desire. The only way to truly please Him is by having faith that He exists and by believing He rewards us when we diligently seek Him. So I began to pray for an increased measure of faith in my life. And with time, I saw my old fears slowly slipping away. When I felt the temptation of fear creeping back into my thoughts, I prayed, "Lord, I gave that issue to you a long time ago. I don't intend on taking it back now. So I am trusting you, Lord, to handle that for me." And the seeds of faith began to slowly grow into the fruit of faith. And they are continually growing to this day, as I carefully cultivate my faith through reading and meditating on God's Word, and through taking time to develop an intimate relationship with my Lord.

> "By faith Noah, when warned about things not yet seen, in holy fear built an ark to save his family. By his faith he condemned the world and became heir of the righteousness that comes from faith."
>
> (Hebrews 11:7)

For some reason, this passage stood out even more than all the others. I kept reading it over and over. I felt that God was trying to tell me something, yet I didn't understand. I felt that I saw the tip of an iceberg of truth, but there was much more to it than I saw. I still feel that way. But as I wrestled with this seemingly insignificant passage, I did see deeper truth than I had originally grasped. You know the story of Noah, who lived in a time where sin was the norm and righteousness was rare. It was so rare, in fact, that only Noah was found to be righteous. How did he stay faithful when the tides of a sinful culture sent constant waves of temptation wherever he went? I think the secret is found in Genesis 6:9: *"This is the account of Noah. Noah was a righteous man, blameless among the people of his time, and he walked with God."*

Noah walked with God. He did not run ahead of God or lag behind Him. He consistently walked with God step by step, day after day. We can learn from that. Sometimes in a winter season of life it is almost easier to walk with God than when everything in life is bright and beautiful. It is because the winter seasons of life reveal our deep need for God—a reality in every season, but one that shouts loud and clear in the winter season. This side of heaven we will not see all the benefits of walking with God. Our earthly eyes cannot comprehend the blessings that automatically come from walking with God. We must trust that God always sees through a wide-angle lens. He sees what we can't see or accomplish. And just because we don't see it, doesn't mean that it is not happening. These truths can be discerned from the simple passage of Hebrews 11:7: *"By faith Noah, when warned about things not yet seen, in holy fear built an ark to save his family. By his faith he condemned the world and became heir of the righteousness that comes from faith."*

Noah obeyed God, believed God, was faithful to God, but he did it for his little family. But God had a much bigger plan in store. Noah only saw and understood a small piece of the puzzle. But God uses imperfect people to bring about His perfect will. God uses the ordinary to bring about the extraordinary. Noah's obedience affects us now. But he didn't see that. And we don't see God's huge, multi-faceted plan in our lives either. We don't see the big picture that what we are doing today affects generations to come. We need to remember that we don't see the big picture. But we need to think about our legacy and "make the most of every opportunity".

Legacy

As I have said, our God is a big God, able to do big things. One example of the ways that God can take a godly effort of leaving behind a godly legacy and make it huge, happened back in the 1950s with a preacher named Peter Marshall, who had a profound impact on those in whom he came into contact. There is a wonderful old movie called "A Man Called Peter" that describes his powerful life. He was a poor immigrant from Scotland who was touched by the Holy Spirit then called to America to preach. He rose from being an immigrant to construction worker, to pastor, to chaplain of the United States Congress. An ordinary person with an extraordinary God! Though he died while still young, he must have had a profound effect on his son, Peter John Marshall, for he grew up to be a powerful evangelist, just like his father.

One winter day, my whole family was relaxing together watching "A Man Called Peter". One of my children asked, "Mom, who is that little boy?" I immediately replied, "Oh that is Peter John, Peter Marshall's son. He grew up to be a great man of God, just like his father." Then I thought for a moment, and suddenly a memory came bursting forth to my mind. I paused the movie, making sure I had everyone's attention, and said, "I'll tell you more about Peter John. He learned from his father about Jesus, and grew up to serve Him. And when I was a little girl, he came to my hometown and preached a sermon at First Presbyterian Church. My mom, Gran to you, went with a friend of hers to hear him even though she was not a member of that church. That night, during his sermon, Gran asked Jesus to be her Savior and the Lord of her life."

Though I was only about eight years old, I still remember the change that took place in my mother, and it had a profound effect on my own life. Her change made me hungry for God. Don't you see? God uses the ordinary to do the extraordinary from generation to generation to generation—from a poor Scottish immigrant to his son, to my mother, to me, to my children and on and on and on. What a mighty God we serve!

I once shared with my brother that my daughter, Ellie, seemed to wrestle with big spiritual issues at such a young age. He replied by saying, "You know what that tells me? That God has big plans for Ellie. It may just be that she will be great grandmother to a great man of God, but the plan must be huge!" We need to believe big things for ourselves and for those we love all because we have an extraordinary God who loves to work in ordinary lives.

And the list of faith-filled God followers continues on in Hebrews 11. It speaks of Abraham and Isaac, and Moses and his parents, and many more—all mentioned in this faith Hall of Fame, simply for the fact that they believed, and this belief was counted as righteousness. They believed in an extraordinary God, who because of their belief did extraordinary things in each of them. Some saw great miracles, and some experienced the even greater miracle of peace and endurance when their actual miracle did not come until much later, even after death.

Chapter 19
Miracles

"But seek first the kingdom of God and His righteousness, and all these things shall be added to you."

(Matthew 6:33; NKJ)

The command is clear. We should seek Him first, above all things. The rest is left in His hands. It is no big deal for God to provide everything that we need, both physically and spiritually. The main thing is that we seek Him. Joshua spent a long time learning this great lesson. He was a youth when the mighty hand of God performed all the great miracles of deliverance as Moses led the people out of Egypt. He saw the plagues, yet was spared. This had to have had an incredible impact on his young heart. He crossed the parted Red Sea on dry land. He ate the manna. He heard the complaints. Yet, all evidence points to a faithful heart. He must have remembered all that he had seen.

We can try to use the excuse that times are different now, harder in fact. We can say that it would have been easier for

Joshua to experience God, to believe and remember, because God worked in bigger ways then. But I just don't buy that excuse. God's Word clearly states in Hebrews 13:8 that our God is the same yesterday, today and forever. Therefore, the same God who parted the Red Sea, who sent forth the 12 plagues, who healed the sick and made the blind to see, has not changed! His power has not changed! Actually, there are miracles all around us, disguised in the ordinary. Have you ever experienced or witnessed the birth of a baby? My grandfather, Robert Kincade, was outwardly a tough man who did not suffer fools, yet he loved to hold his great grandchildren and carefully examine their tiny hands and feet. He recognized the miracle placed in his lap.

Have you ever heard of or experienced the joy of adoption? It is a miracle to see a family made complete by a perfect stranger. What a beautifully reflective and descriptive view of our place in the heart our heavenly Father!

> *"But when the fullness of the time came, God sent forth His Son, born of a woman, born under the Law, so that He might redeem those who were under the Law, that we might receive the adoption of sons. And because you are sons, God has sent forth the Spirit of His Son into our hearts, crying, "Abba! Father!"* (Galatians 4:4-6; NAS)

When we ask Jesus to be our Lord and Savior, we are adopted into the family of God.

There are many other miracles which occur in our daily lives. What about those times that you missed having a wreck by a fraction of a turn? Do you not see that a mighty hand was involved? All of these are miracles wrapped up in the ordinary.

One summer day I was serving lunch to my children. We had just given thanks for the food and the children began to dive into their PB&J sandwiches. Suddenly, my daughter Ellie, who was four years old at the time, stopped eating and said urgently, "Mama, we need to pray for Daddy." So, we all stopped eating and said a simple prayer of blessing and protection for my husband, Mont. Five minutes later the phone rang. It was Mont. He said that he had just been involved in a "fender-bender," but was not hurt. As he described the accident, we both realized that it had the potential to be much more tragic, but that God had offered His mercy and protection once again. We believe that God prompted Ellie to pray at just the right moment, because of her pure, child-like faith.

Trial by Fire

Another miraculous moment came when I was a senior in college. You must understand that the miracle came at a time that I felt that God had been silent in my life—one of those quiet seasons that we can't feel Him, or see Him, or hear Him in our lives, no matter how much we seek and pray. Those times can seem to last forever. But, it is during those times that faith, in its purest form must step in. Hebrews 11:1 states that *"Faith is being sure of what we hope for, confident of what we do not see..."* In hindsight, it was a short season that God used to test my faith and to prepare me for His glory about to be revealed. It was during that time that God was faithfully carrying me; I just didn't realize it at the time.

Over the Christmas holiday of my senior year, I had developed an infection which quickly turned into a chronic state, probably due to four years of neglecting my health. I ended up having to drop out of school for that last semester, which meant that I could not graduate with my class. I went on to graduate the next semester, but graduating on time had been a goal which I had not been able to achieve. It was because of this change of plans I was able to do mission work in Costa Rica, which so completely changed my life. But I didn't know that then. Along with other situations which seem small now, but huge then, I began to feel that perhaps God had forgotten about me. Yet, it was during that time that I learned to praise Him for who He is, not just for what He does.

One particular Saturday afternoon, my roommate Larren and I were getting ready to go out for lunch when we both heard loud popping noises. We both laughed, thinking that it was our neighbor, Mark, trying to play a trick on us as he often did. But when we went into the den we saw black smoke quickly filling the room. We ran to the door and felt it. It was warm, but not too hot, so we opened the door to try to get out of the apartment. The wind was blowing the flames across the doorway so we were unable to get out that way. By now the flames had reached our curtains in the den. We ran to the back bedroom in the apartment and realized that we would have to jump out of the second-story bedroom window. Larren went first and landed safely on the ground. I climbed out the window, and as I hung there smoke was billowing out of one vent on the right side of me, and flames were coming out of another vent on the left side of me. I have never liked heights, so dropping from the window of the second floor was not an easy task. Larren kept calling for me to let go of the ledge and I kept hesitating, afraid of what would happen when I let go. I just hung there saying desperate prayers out loud, and finally, when my arms got too tired to hang on any longer, I just let go.

. The fall was quick and not too painful. I limped away from the apartment building, wanting to get as far away from it as possible. Someone must have called the fire department, because within a couple of minutes we heard the sirens coming. The fire was put out fairly quickly, and after a while we were allowed to go inside and assess the damage. When we went into the den we saw that the curtains and couch had burned up and the walls were all charred. I turned to close the door and something caught my eye. There was a small piece of paper which had been taped above the door. My friend, Kelli, had placed it there before she moved to another city. It had been there for so long that I did not even notice it anymore—until that moment. It stood out so prominently because of its stark contrast to the black walls. You see, the edges of the paper were charred, but the paper had not burned. And the words on the paper were as clear as they ever had been—even clearer because of the truth that they pronounced so loudly. The paper had a scripture typed on it, which read: *"Just as the mountains surround and protect Jerusalem, so the Lord surrounds his people..."* (Psalms 125:2; NLT).

Larrin, the taller of the two of us, reached up and took the scripture from the wall. There was a tan square left there reminding us of what color the walls used to be, and reminding us that our God was and is still the God of miracles.

Where are you in your journey of faith? Are you in a burning building that you don't even realize is on fire? If this is where you are, let me say that you have a friend, Jesus, who wants to save you from your destruction. Or have you realized that where you are is a dangerous situation, but have not found the way out yet? If this is where you are, I want you to know that you have a friend, Jesus, who will guide you to a safe and abundant place. Or maybe you are trying to get out, still hanging on to the ledge, but are scared to let go. You may continue to hang there until your arms get so tired of hanging on that you have to let go. Let me encourage you to go ahead and let go. You have a friend, Jesus, who will catch you. He can be trusted. I know because I have experienced Him for myself. And maybe you are already safely out of the burning building. You are safe in the arms of Jesus. But what of the others who have not yet found safety? What is your role in their lives?

I once had a dream: my husband Mont and I were sitting at an outdoor café enjoying a relaxing lunch together. Suddenly, someone came up to us and said, "The children are in the burning building. Will you help get the children out of the burning building?" We immediately said yes, and then the scene switched to inside the building. It was like a hotel or apartment complex. There was no smoke and no flames, but we knew that there was an urgency to get the "children" out of this "burning" building. We devised a system in which I would go down the hallway and gather the "children" and bring them to Mont, who would put them in the elevator and take them all the way out of the building. Interestingly, these "children" were not just children—they were young, old and middle-aged; people of different ages, races and social standings.

As I came back with more of these "children," I saw that Mont had set up a concession stand and was selling snacks to the people gathered. I said, "Mont, the building is on fire! We have to get the people out of the building!" He said, "Oh, yea! I forgot!" and then began his work again, taking the children safely out of the building. I came back with more people and Mont was in the elevator. I knew that it was the last elevator out. Mont was in the elevator, talking, laughing and being very charming to these people who I knew to be very important in the eyes of the world. I stood there watching the doors to the elevator close and I realized that he had forgotten once again about what his mission truly was. When I woke up, what immediately came to my mind was "love of money" and "pride of life". I discussed the dream with Mont, explaining what I felt that I needed to learn from it.

Maybe the dream was due to too much pizza the night before, but as I reflected on it I pondered the thought that we as Christians often forget that this brief life is like a burning building. Maybe we are already safe and secure because we have already experienced the saving grace of Jesus. But for the rest of the world, it is as if they are in a burning building and they don't realize the urgency to get out of it, and run to the safety of the loving arms of Christ. And we Christians often get so distracted with the love of money, our material possessions, and the pride of life—seeking to please the rest of the world instead of our Father, that we forget what our mission truly is. And, we forget how short the time is that we have to complete our mission. We must keep our eyes on Jesus, the author and one who perfects our faith. He left heaven to come to earth, the burning building, to be the way out. We as Christians just need to point others to the way out.

"Blessed be the God and Father of our Lord Jesus Christ, who according to His great mercy has caused us to be born again to a living hope through the resurrection of Jesus Christ from the dead, to obtain an inheritance which is imperishable and undefiled and will not fade away, reserved in heaven for you, who are protected by the power of God through faith for a salvation ready to be revealed in the last time.

In this you greatly rejoice, even though now for a little while, if necessary, you have been distressed by various trials, that the proof of your faith, being more precious than gold which is perishable, even though tested by fire, may be found to result in praise and glory and honor at the revelation of Jesus Christ; and though you have not seen Him, you love Him, and though you do not see Him now, but believe in Him, you greatly rejoice with joy inexpressible and full of glory, obtaining as the outcome of your faith the salvation of your souls." (1Peter 1:3-9; NAS)

Chapter 20
Order of the Seasons

Hanna Hurnard wrote a beautiful, anointed allegory back in 1955. The truth of this allegory defies time, and the story has touched my life in this 21st Century as it did anyone who may have read it in the 1950s. The story is called *Hinds Feet on High Places*, and it teaches about the ups and downs of our journey with Christ Jesus. The allegory is centered on a little girl named Much-Afraid. She lived in the Valley of Despair until she met the Great Shepherd who promised to lead her to the wonderful High Places. He promised to be with her the whole time, though at times she wouldn't be able to see Him. Her guides were named Sorrow and Suffering and if she learned to take their hands, the way would be easier.

All along the journey, she would see paths that appeared to be the easy way up. Yet her guides kept taking her along the rough places. Yet it was through these rough paths that she was gradually able to surrender different parts of herself, which not only healed her but also brought glory to the Great Shepherd.

Near the end of her journey, she realized that the time had come for her to surrender her whole heart. She knew it might be painful, yet she climbed upon the altar willingly. She only asked one thing: "Please tie my hands so I won't fight you." Soon after she surrendered her whole heart, she reached the beautiful High Places.

I have thought a lot about this dear story. I think it so strikes a chord in my heart because in so many ways I am that crippled little girl named Much-Afraid. And I'm heading for the heights, yet so often I have to pray, "Please help me not to fight You." But you see I have tasted enough of the best to realize that nothing else can make me satisfied, whole and healed. And though the route is not always the easiest, it is definitely the best. In his book, *The Story of the Other Wise Man*, Henry Van Dyke states:

> *"It is better to follow even the shadow of the best than to remain content with the worst. And those who would see wonderful things must often be ready to travel alone."*xii

And perhaps that is true. We often feel so alone in our winter seasons of life. However, we can sing boldly, "Though none go with me, still I will follow," for we have learned the magnificent secret: We are never truly alone, for the One who matters has promised to never leave us nor forsake us.

Most often, our places of surrender come in the form of a crossroads of life. Difficult circumstances lead us to a spot in the road of faith where we have a decision to make. We can choose the path of bitterness or we can choose to *"trust*

in the Lord with all of your heart and lean not on your own understand-
ing" (Prov. 3:5-6). This type of trust—when we just don't
understand—is a type of sacrifice on the altar of faith. It is a
choosing to believe, despite what we can see. It is remembering
what we know about God and who He really is, even when our
circumstances don't seem to be displaying evidence of the truth
that we know.

Second Timothy 1:12 says, *"for I know whom I have believed and*
am persuaded that He is able to keep what I have committed to Him until
that Day" (NKJ). This requires relationship, and a very personal
one. It is not just facts about God, it is experience with God. It
is friendship. It is spending time together daily. It is daily trust
which leads to difficult trust. It is extraordinary, a miracle actually, when that point of surrender to what we want and what we
truly think we need takes us to a point of peace in the midst of
the difficult circumstances. And we must remember that our
extraordinary God is also the resurrection God. He is the God
of new life. Winter will always come in every life. But the truth
that we must hold on to is that spring is just around the corner,
when we put our trust in Him, leaning not upon our own understanding.

Remember

It was March of 1987. My dear friend, Lisa, and I were living in Memphis. We had transferred to another college for the
spring semester in order to work with the youth group that I
had worked with for three summers. Little did I know that God
had called me there for me, not for the youth group. A devastating event was about to take place, and because of His great

love for me He had orchestrated where I needed to be as the event came trickling through the filter of His love. When the call came, I was alone. I knelt on the floor of the living room of the house that Lisa and I lived in on the church property. I stayed in that prayer position for a very long time, yet not one word came to my mouth or even to my mind. I didn't know what to say. Fear and grief had captured my heart, silencing every word that I longed to pray. Yet, when I got up off the floor, I knew that I had prayed. And I knew that God had heard. I felt His presence. He had heard my heart, and He was with me. I still felt weak and fearful, but I could move. However, the battle to comprehend the situation continued in my mind…

Oh, God, not Hess!

Maybe it is not like they think it is.

Maybe it will all turn out all right.

Surely God would not take another friend.

Two were buried last week due to another terrible accident.

That can't happen again, can it?

Statistics alone would say that the chances are on my side.

But this is real life, not statistical numbers on paper.

You can't predict real life.

All these thoughts repeatedly flew across my mind. And then I would think about Hess, my oldest friend. Our families had been friends for generations, since before our ancestors had moved together to our small town in 1876. Growing up, we spent many Friday nights together. Our families went on vacations together. We went to camp together. I had just seen her the week before when we were both home for spring break. Not Hess. I couldn't even imagine her injured, or worse, because she was full of more life than any person I knew. Hess was all about laughter and joy.

The next 15 hours were a blur spent at the hospital, The Med in Memphis; the long night talking with Allen, Hess' first cousin and as close to me as a sister. It was almost a holy time as we shared every memory we could think of Hess. We laughed and we cried. Laughter through tears, the tenderest emotion there is, as Allen says.

And then suddenly, it was over; no more tests to wait on; Just a funeral to attend. As I drove alone back to the house, loud and unreal great sobs came from the deepest part of me.

Oh, God, not Hess.

My mind couldn't even wrap around the thought that she was gone. When I arrived home, I went straight to the bathroom to splash cold water on my face.

I gotta pull myself together.

I washed my face, and then looked up into the mirror. The same words as a prayer came again...

Oh, God, not Hess.

As the tears came again, I whispered another prayer...

God, help me.

As I looked back into the mirror, a memory flashed through my mind; One that I had not thought of the night before. It was so clear and vivid it almost startled me.

How could I have forgotten that?

We were in middle school and had traveled with my youth group to Kentucky for a weekend event called Icthus, a Christian "Woodstock". We stayed in tents and spent the weekend listening to cool Christian musicians and great speakers. The last night I sat by Hess as we listened to a powerful speaker talk of a personal relationship with Christ. I had already had that priceless experience of meeting the Savior, though I had a lot to learn about Jesus being my Lord. Afterwards, Hess wanted to talk to me. We went into the large counseling tent and sat down on the fold-up chairs. Hess wanted to know what I thought of the speaker's words. I explained to her my own personal experience as young as it was. It was the first time I had ever talked to anyone except my parents about my relationship with Christ.

Hess said that she wanted a relationship with Christ, too. I went to get a counselor to talk with her, and then waited on the back row while they talked and prayed. Hess was beaming when she walked back to where I was sitting. She told me that she had done it! She was now a follower of Christ Jesus.

As I stood there in front of that mirror, remembering the greatest event of Hess' 21 years, a powerful peace flooded my heart and soul. I actually smiled because I was going to be O.K. I would see Hess again. I was there when her heavenly home was secured. And one day we'd be there together. Of course, the following months were very painful. But after that holy time of remembrance, which came as a direct answer to my cry for help, my tears were not for Hess. I cried many tears for myself, for Allen, for Hess' parents, for all of her family, but I had no need to cry for Hess. Hess was just fine; better than fine, she was home.

Easter came just two weeks after Hess died. It was the most painful springtime I had ever experienced. But it stands out in my mind as the Easter that I "got it". I finally understood that Jesus understands. He, too, hanging on the cross, full of pain and grief on our behalf, cried, *"My God, my God why have you for-saken me?"* (Matt. 27:46b). Yes, of course, that signified who He was—the fulfillment of the prophesy of Psalm 22, which begins with the same words. But I believe He not only fulfilled those words, He felt those words. And I understood much better what it cost Him in the garden when He prayed, *"My Father, if it is pos-sible, let this cup pass from Me; yet not as I will, but as You will"* (Matt. 26:39; NAS). I finally understood that Jesus understands. And because He is a big God, the Creator of my emotions, He could handle any emotions that I felt. It was safe to share all of my emotions with Him, no matter how "unholy" they seemed.

And suddenly, I understood the resurrection. It now was not just a fact that would someday gain eternal bliss for me. It was real now. It meant that I would laugh with Hess again. Our God is a resurrection God. He takes the death inside of us and around us and He brings new life. Eternal springtime, beginning the moment we surrender to His lordship, and lasting for eternity; Even if, for a season, we can't see it or feel it. But we must remember the order of things, practically and spiritually. Springtime always follows winter. It's how it works. Our winter seasons of life prepare the soil of our hearts to see the extraordinary working of our extraordinary God. If there was no winter season, there would be no springtime.

Spring

I love the time spent in my big green chair during the springtime. Oh, the joy that comes when the first buds are spotted! How perfectly ordered it is that springtime should follow winter. After the long, cold winter, those first signs of green grass, small flowers, and birds singing bring an energy and excitement to my soul. The old has gone, the new has come! It has happened once again! The sun shines brightly and warmly, the colors come forth vibrantly. Spring is a reminder that all of His promises are yes and amen! All of God's Word is tried and true. God always wins. Therefore, if He is living in us, He is winning through us, if we are following Him and walking in His ways.

Springtime burst forth in my own life one year in a very dramatic way. In the late '80s and early '90s, I taught first grade at a small Christian school in Memphis. The children were a great source of joy to me, and often I learned more from them than they did from me. I had been teaching the children in our daily devotions to pray about everything, and that yes, indeed, God did hear and answer our prayers. Often I allowed different students to come forward in the class and pray aloud for the concerns that we had discussed. As is often the case, my lessons were soon put to the test.

A precious little blond-headed girl named Coley came to class one morning with a beautiful butterfly in a jar. We all oohed and aahed over the magnificent colors of the butterfly. Coley was quick to point out to everyone that the butterfly had a broken wing. Upon inspection, I could plainly see that a large portion of one of the wings was not just broken, but completely torn off. We placed the jar with the butterfly on the shelf so that everyone could see it. It remained there for most of the morning. During my break, I went to the prayer room at the church. I locked the door and knelt before my Lord, and poured out my heart. You see, I was in a winter stage of my life. One of those cold, lonely times that you can't see clearly how God could possibly bring about all those great and wonderful things that He promises to those who believe and follow Him. I don't even remember all of the details of that hard time, and it has been so completely healed that the pain is only a distant memory now. On that day, however, I felt pain and confusion so greatly that I spent my entire break kneeling before the Lord, begging to know His presence in my life.

When I returned to the classroom, we began our Bible lesson. One of the children suggested that we pray for Coley's butterfly. Not wanting to retract my admonition that we should bring every concern before the Lord in prayer, I consented to a prayer time for the butterfly. I asked for volunteers to come forward to pray aloud for the butterfly and three-fourths of the class quickly stepped to the front ready to pray. As the children began to pray, my heart started racing. I shot up silent prayers like: "Lord, get me out of this! Give me wisdom in explaining this to these dear children!" You see, the faith-filled prayers of those first graders were: "Lord, please heal the butterfly!" and "Please help the butterfly to fly again!" When all had prayed and were returning to their seats, one little boy suggested that we let the butterfly "get some fresh air". Why I consented I will never know, but before I even realized what was taking place the whole class had stepped outside to the grassy courtyard right outside our classroom.

When Coley emptied the butterfly from the jar onto the grass, I felt immediate regret in having allowed this to take place. The butterfly just jumped around on the grass. The sight brought pity and sadness and regret. I quickly ushered the children back inside, leaving the butterfly in the grass. I began a math lesson to try to take their minds off the butterfly, but I kept seeing various children glancing out the window checking on the still-hopping butterfly. I was in the middle of the very ineffective math lesson when one of the boys stepped away from his seat to look out of the window. He gasped and yelled, "Look!" Everyone rushed from their seats to the window just in time to see the butterfly lift off the ground in flight. The children began to yell and scream and laugh and cheer and hug, all in pure joy of seeing answered prayer. One of the other first-grade teachers came rushing in to see what all the commotion was about. All I could do was point out the window at the butterfly, which was now flying all over the courtyard.

We stood looking in amazement until the butterfly flew over the wall of the courtyard past our visibility. Then, I once again asked for volunteers to pray. Everyone joined in this time, especially me. We thanked God for His miracle of love, healing and answered prayer. And for me, my winter season of life began to quickly lift. You see, I felt like a butterfly with a broken wing. I was a Christian; I had already obtained new life, which is so allegorically portrayed through the life of a butterfly. But painful circumstances had rendered me incapable of flying to the heights that God had planned for me. I, too, needed the healing touch of the Great Physician. I needed to see and feel His presence. And when I surrendered to Him in the prayer room, when I trusted Him despite what I could see, He showed me His presence in a way that was far greater than I could have ever imagined. Are you a butterfly with a broken wing? Call upon the Father, the Great Physician, to heal you so that you can fly to the heights of His beautiful plan for your life.

Everyone has scars. That is life's reality. That will continue to be life's reality until Jesus comes back, or we head to our heavenly home. But scars can fade with proper healing. And no counselor, no self-help book, no medication can heal completely—only Jesus, the Great Physician. When you surrender to the lordship of Jesus in every area of your life, the surrender does not give you a barrier from the pain or the scars. But it does give you automatic access to the great I Am; to the Wonderful Counselor, Mighty God, Prince of Peace; to Emmanuel, which means "God With Us". Jesus is always there to comfort and to heal and to assure us that we are not alone.

Conclusion: Stones of Remembrance

We began this book with Joshua. I don't know about you, but I have come to see him as a dear friend. We began our study with his shining moment of glory: finally leading the people into the Promised Land. A former slave now anointed leader. And then we worked our way backwards to his time of mentorship with Moses, when he could continually be found in the tent of meeting worshiping. And we recalled his time of military leadership, fighting the Amalekites. We talked about the meaning of his name, and saw many ways that he was simply an ordinary man, prepared by God for an extraordinary work. And that preparation began even before he was born.

Do you remember when Joseph (coat of many colors Joseph) took his two sons, Ephraim and Manasseh to the death bed of his father Jacob to be blessed? And do you remember what Jacob did? He crossed his arms placing the right hand of blessing, usually reserved for the first born on Ephraim's head. The name Manasseh was significant in indicating a very painful past. The name Ephraim, the second born, was indicative of a fruitful future. When Jacob crossed his arms, he was making a bold statement. He was saying from that day forward the fruitfulness of the future would take precedence over the pain of the past. And what a true proclamation that was. Not only in Ephraim's lifetime, but also in his future descendants. Our dear friend Joshua was a descendent of Ephraim.

In fact, in the first chapter I told you to watch for certain holy numbers such as three, seven, 12, and 40. Forty is often a number of cleansing and preparation for the extraordinary. The number three can be classified as holy perfection. Seven indicates completion and perfection. Twelve often encompasses the family of God, represents all God's people, and reminds us of the covenant or unending promises of God for His people. Joshua was the 12th generation from Ephraim. He was Ephraim's great-to-the-12th grandson! The fruitfulness continued on in a mighty way!

When we began this book, we found Joshua gathering stones. The purpose of the stones was as stones of remembrance. At the Lord's command, Joshua said to the people.

> *"In the future when your descendants ask their fathers, 'What do these stones mean? Tell them, 'Israel crossed the Jordan on dry ground.' For the Lord your God dried up the Jordan before you until you had crossed over. The Lord your God did to the Jordan just what he had done to the Red Sea when he dried it up before us until we had crossed over. He did this so that all the peoples of the earth might know that the hand of the Lord is powerful and so that you might always fear the Lord your God."* (Joshua 4:21-24)

The Lord wanted them to take the stones from the Jordan because he knew so well that they were a forgetful people. They were forgetful about who He is, what He can do and what He requires. So for the rest of Joshua's life, He was called to remember. Joshua gathered the stones from the River Jordan as they entered the Promised Land, which was just the beginning. As we continue studying about Joshua, we find that throughout his time of leadership he was called to gather stones of remembrance seven different times. The seventh time that Joshua was called to gather stones of remembrance was just before his death.

1. Joshua 4:20—Stones from the River Jordan

2. Joshua 7:26—Large pile of rocks gathered as a memorial of how they weeded out sin and evil from among the people.

3. Joshua 8:29—Large pile of rocks gathered as a memorial of victory over their enemies.

4. Joshua 8:32—Gathered large stones and copied the commandments as a memorial of renewed decision to follow God.

5. Joshua 10:27—A pile of stones gathered to cover their defeated enemies.

6. Joshua 22:31—Built an altar of stones as a testimony and reminder that the people and their future generations would stay true to God.

7. Joshua 24:26—Gathered all the people together to remember their great journey, and to renew their covenant with God.

We have already studied the first episode when they gathered the stones from the River Jordan. Now, let's look at the last time Joshua was called to gather stones. This is found in Joshua 23 and 24.

Joshua's Farewell to the Leaders

"After a long time had passed and the LORD had given Israel rest from all their enemies around them, Joshua, by then old and well advanced in years, summoned all Israel—their elders, leaders, judges and officials—and said to them: "I am old and well advanced in years. You yourselves have seen everything the LORD your God has done to all these nations for your sake; it was the LORD your God who fought for you. Remember..."

(Joshua 23:1-3)

And then Joshua began to instruct the people for the last time. This is what he told them: *"Be very strong: be careful to obey all that is written in the Book of the Law of Moses, without turning aside to the right or to the left"* (Josh. 23:6). Compare that to what Joshua heard over and over from the Lord himself, when He first became leader:

"Be strong and very courageous. Be careful to obey all the law my servant Moses gave you; do not turn from it to the right or to the left, that you may be successful wherever you go...Have I not commanded

you? Be strong and courageous. Do not be terrified; do not be dis-
couraged, for the LORD your God will be with you wherever
you go."   (Josh. 1:7, 9)

He passed the wisdom on to the others. And that wisdom
had been tested and proved throughout his lifetime. And he
goes on to give more instruction:

"But you are to hold fast to the LORD your God, as you have until
now. The LORD has driven out before you great and powerful nations;
to this day no one has been able to withstand you. One of you routs
a thousand, because the LORD your God fights for you, just as he
promised. So be very careful to love the LORD your God…You
know with all your heart and soul that not one of all the good promises
the Lord your God gave you has failed. Every promise has been
fulilled; not one has failed."   (Joshua 23:8-11, 14)

And then he gathered all the people together, and he called
them to remember the great journey on which God had led
them. Then he challenged them, through remembering, to
renew their covenant. He said, *"…choose for yourselves this day whom*
you will serve…But as for me and my household, we will serve the Lord"
(Josh. 24:15).

The people renewed their covenant to their faithful God.
And then Joshua called them to action. They were to do two
things:
1. They were to throw away and rid themselves from all
    false gods.
2. They were to yield their hearts to the Lord.

And the people enthusiastically agreed. Joshua drew up a "plan of obedience"...decrees and laws. And he took a large stone and he set it up under the oak, as a stone of remembrance of their moment of decision to follow the Lord wholeheartedly.

This proved to be Joshua's final assignment from God. He died right after setting up this final stone of remembrance. With this seventh stone, Joshua could rest. Seven being the number of completeness and perfection signified that with this last stone, Joshua had completed his ministry. Sounds much like Paul wrote in 2 Timothy 4:7: *"I have fought the good fight, I have finished the race, I have kept the faith."*

With these seven different piles of stones of remembrance scattered throughout the land, the land itself shouted the story of God's faithful promises: the wonderful Promised Land. We can understand with greater clarity the encounter with Jesus found in Luke 19: 37-40:

"When he came near the place where the road goes down the Mount of Olives, the whole crowd of disciples began joyfully to praise God in loud voices for all the miracles they had seen:

"'Blessed is the king who comes in the name of the Lord!'
'Peace in heaven and glory in the highest!'

"Some of the Pharisees in the crowd said to Jesus, 'Teacher, rebuke your disciples!'

'I tell you,' he replied, 'if they keep quiet, the stones will cry out.'"

Joshua learned most of all to remember who God is, what He has and can do. To remember that He is an extraordinary God who loves to work in the lives of ordinary people.

All of this reflection and revelation pours forth on ordinary days in the life of an ordinary person. Some may say that they don't have that sweet intimacy. But I believe with all that I am that you too can have the indescribable joy and strength, and peace, and abundant life that I and many others have found. Just ask and you will receive. Just listen and you will hear the whisper of the Holy Spirit in your soul. Just look for Him, He is not hiding. He is calling to you to find Him and all that He longs to give you. Just take time to sit in your own big, green chair, and:

Reach up….
Reach out…
And always Remember…

It is the stones of remembrance—the remembering—that will especially give you strength through every season of your faith walk. And that is what life is all about—remembering that in my ordinary life, there is a living, active and extraordinary God!

Endnotes

i The Autobiography of Charles H. Spurgeon, New York, NY, Fleming H. Revell Co., 1898, I: 102 - 104.

ii Ibid

iii Ibid

iv Ibid

v Ibid

vi Ibid

vii The New International Version Study Bible, Grand Rapids, Michigan, Zondervan, 1973, 1978, 1984 International Bible Society: 718, 1410, 674.

viii Purpose Driven Life, Grand Rapids, Michigan, Zondervan, 2002 Rick Warren: 17.

ix One Year Book of Praying Through the Bible, Carol Stream, Illinois, Tyndale House, 2003 Cheri Fuller.

x The New International Version Study Bible, Grand Rapids, Michigan, Zondervan, 1973, 1978, 1984 International Bible Society: 718, 1410, 674.

xi Ibid

xii The Story of the Other Wiseman, London, Harper and Brothers Publishers, 1900, 29.

xiii Stuart, Unity and Diversity, July 24, 2009, http://talk.thinkmatters.org.

Sara W. Berry

Sara W. Berry, author and creator of many Bethel Road products, has been teaching, be it in a classroom setting or church setting, for the past 17 years. Her experience began at Millsaps College in Jackson, Mississippi where she received a Bachelor of Science Degree in Education, as well as numerous education and leadership awards.

Her varied work experience includes teaching elementary students in Memphis, TN; Nashville, TN; Jackson, MS; Costa Rica and Ecuador. She was director of a tutorial program for inner city children in Jackson, MS as well as program director for an inner city humanitarian service in Memphis, TN. She also served as children's director for her church in Tupelo, MS.

She is married to Dr. Mont Berry and her teaching experience continues each day as she is rearing her five children: Katie, Ellie, Joseph, Troy and Joshua.

Sara has an intense love for discipleship. She desires to teach, through her books and curriculum, the truth of God's Word, knowing that the Word does not return void. Sara has an equal passion for missions. She has taken seriously the mandate of the Great Commission. She lived in San Jose, Costa Rica as a missionary teacher in the late 1980s. After her marriage to Mont, they both lived in Shell Mera, Ecuador, he working at a jungle hospital, she teaching at the Nate Saint Memorial School. Most recently, the entire Berry family spent time in mission service in Trujillo, Peru. In recent years, Sara also spent time in China. At present, several of Sara's programs are being translated into Spanish, Chinese and Hindi.

With the gift of teaching, and a passion for discipleship, Sara Berry finds great joy in sharing the truth of the Scriptures with others. Sara has shared her material from *Stones from the River Jordan* with hundreds of women from the United States, South America and China. If you are interested in scheduling a speaking engagement, or for information on any other books or teaching materials by Sara Berry, email us at **info@bethelroadpublications.com**.

Stones from the River Jordan is also available in an 8-Week Bible Study Audio Series taught by Sara Berry. A study guide accompanies the series. This *Stones from the River Jordan Study Guide* is also available separately for personal reflection while reading the book. Check out our website for these and other materials.

www.bethelroadpublications.com